Free at Last

by

Rod Parsley

Columbus, Ohio

Unless otherwise indicated, all Scripture quotations are taken from the *King James Version* of the Bible.

Free at Last

ISBN 1-880244-18-7
Copyright 1994 by Rod Parsley
Published by:
Results Publishing
P.O. Box 32932
Columbus, Ohio 43232-0932 USA

TABLE OF CONTENTS

Introduction

There's a Devil Loose!

There is a war going on around you between the ministering spirits of God and the spirits of darkness, and they are fighting over your life!

Demon spirits are frenzied and running loose in these last days, and they are out to destroy you, your family, your home and your nation.

America is rolling in luxury, reveling in pleasure and rotting in sin. Passions run amok like riderless horses. Lust is exalted as lord. Sin is treated as sovereignty and Satan is worshipped as a saint.

From perverted politicians who promote godless legislation to the street punk with an assault rifle, to the so-called solid citizen who shakes his fist at the commandments of a holy God ... America is possessed!

This onslaught of evil is too sinister and too subtle to be the work of human origin. It is the carefully calculated conspiracy of demonic entities.

Doctrines of Devils

Twisted teaching has crept into the church. Just as the apostle Paul warned would happen in the last days:

Now the Spirit speaketh expressly that in the latter times some shall depart from the faith, giving heed to seducing spirits, and doctrines of devils (1 Timothy 4:1).

We don't call sin "sin" any longer. Now we call it "a problem" and send the person to a psychologist.

A murderer is no longer a heinous criminal. He is just a victim of society, born on the wrong side of the tracks. He was deprived of the right socioeconomic opportunities. He is the real victim.

Adultery is no longer considered sin in Hollywood ... or in 90 percent of the church world. Movies and television never show any of the disastrous consequences. The audience never gets even a hint that AIDS exists.

Teenage sexual activity will result in nearly 1,000,000 pregnancies annually, leading to 406,000 abortions, 134,000 miscarriages and 490,000 live births. About 3,000,000 teens will contract a sexually transmitted disease. [1]

Half the marriages in this nation end in divorce. Even in the church the divorce rate is keeping pace with the rest of America!

Alcoholism is no longer considered sin. Instead, the alcoholic has a "disease" we spend millions of dollars in advertising each year to propagate. We put a state funded liquor store on one corner and a rehab center on the other!

The President of the United States promised us a cabinet that "looks like America." Twenty-five percent of Americans claim to be evangelical Christians.[2] But how many have been put in high-level government positions? Absolutely none.

Doctrines of humanism and modernistic theology erode the very fiber of the Word of God. Churches have sold out to accommodate the world's decaying values. They no longer believe in the blood. They no longer believe in the Cross. They no longer believe in the virgin birth.

I am not talking about philosophies. I am not talking about ideas, tendencies or sociological trends. I am talking about what the Bible calls "demon spirits," dispatched from the realm of the supernatural to afflict the lives God so lovingly designed and created.

There is a devil loose!

Teen suicide is the third leading cause of death among adolescents.[3] Between 1960 and 1990 the rate of teen suicide increased 400 percent.[4] When our children — living in our homes and attending our churches — are tormented in their minds and driven to take their lives, there is a devil loose!

When the public school systems ban the Bible and use tax dollars to pass out condoms, there is a devil loose!

When 28% of all babies in America are born to single mothers, there is a devil loose![5]

An average of 4,300 babies are torn from their mother's wombs every day while pro-life protesters are thrown into jail.[6]

Animal rights activists are hailed as compassionate heroes, but the slaughter of unborn infants is regarded as a fundamental constitutional right. There is a devil loose!

We do not need another social program. We do not need another government policy. We do not need another self-help psychology book.

We need to recognize there is a devil loose.

The Root of the Problem

When the children of Israel suffered in Egyptian bondage they cried out to God to set them free. God heard their cries and raised up Moses as their deliverer. But God didn't send Moses to confront the children of Israel. He sent Moses to confront Pharaoh.

Pharaoh was the oppressor.

The devil, working through Pharaoh, was the root of their problem.

The devil is the root of our problem today.

The spirit of antichrist is in the world now. The blinding, darkening, deceiving, diabolically deadening power of the devil is overtaking America.

Christians are not immune — we are prime targets. Just because we are saved, the devil does not give up quietly and go away. I believe when we wade into the flow of God's presence, we start jerking the devil's chain. He is angry and he wants to kill you!

When irritation is high and patience is low, know that Satan has come in great wrath. He will try to plague your mind with fear and grotesque images flashing and burning within you. He will try to rob you of restful sleep, drain you of your peace and lay a dark cloud of oppression on your back.

Does worry torment your mind? Do you cringe in fear? Does it seem as though the entire world has gone mad?

Know that spiritual wickedness in high places have come to destroy your life. (Ephesians 6:12.) *The thief cometh not, but for to steal, and to kill, and to destroy (John 10:10).*

We have to confront the oppressor. We have to stand up to the devil.

Standing Up to the Devil

Freedom is never granted by the oppressor. It must be demanded by the oppressed.

The devil will never loosen his stranglehold on your life because you think he should. The devil will never loosen his death grip on your loved ones because it is the right thing to do. He will steal your children, ruin your marriage, wreck your body, rob your bank account and destroy your neighborhood <u>unless</u> you stand up to him.

You have to stand up to him with the authority given to you by Jesus Christ if you are going to break the power of demonic entities.

I have determined to defeat the devil's demonic hosts. I have determined to overthrow the onslaught of the alien armies of the Antichrist that are assailing our lives. It is time to stand up to the powers of darkness and say, "Stop it! In Jesus' name, demon spirits, go!"

I hate Satan and I hate what he does in you. But I know there is power in the Cross of Calvary to set you free.

I am tired of the devil stealing your finances, stealing your joy, stealing your peace and stealing your prosperity. I am tired of watching the body of Christ roll over and become a doormat for the devil.

Jesus did not shed His blood on Calvary for you to submit to the devil. Jesus did not rise in power from the dead for you to only live in bondage and fear. Jesus did not declare, *I am He that liveth, and was dead; and behold, I am alive for evermore (Revelation 1:18)* for the church to live in misery and defeat while the devil laughs.

I am tired of your family being lost! I am tired of you being tormented by illness. Don't allow the devil to deceive you into thinking that you have to be tormented in any area of your life.

It is time to find the devil's minions. It is time to track them down and expose them for what they are. And after we expose them, we are going to cast them out of our lives, our families, our city and our nation.

Cast them out? Yes! It is time for the church of Jesus Christ to march forward, not to be conquered but to conquer, in the name of Christ. It is time to put on our armor and go forth in power to subdue kingdoms, dethrone powers, trample the devil and declare, "We are the church, against which the gates of hell will not prevail!" (Matthew 16:18.)

"They Shall Cast Out Devils"

Jesus said, *These signs shall follow them that believe; In my name shall they cast out devils (Mark 16:17).*

He was talking about you!

Jesus said we would cast out devils. The power to break the strongholds of evil is available to you. But if you are going to go forth in His name, with His authority, to set His people free, you must <u>first</u> be free yourself.

The devil wants you bound. He does not want you free, and he does not want you to set anyone else free.

I believe in living in victory. In fact, I believe in living in victory every minute. We are not called to be discouraged, dismayed or defeated. We are called to be overcomers!

To be an overcomer, you have to enter the fight.

For the church of Jesus Christ to have an impact upon our society, we must go into the battle. God is calling the body of Christ to rise far above the status quo of "church as normal."

We have lived so long in a society where wrong has been right that righteous, holy living has become abnormal. All around us, people are bound and powerless to set themselves free. They do not know who to listen to. They do not know right from wrong.

Millions are careening helplessly on their way to splitting open the bowels of hell, and they cannot see the danger they are in. The crisis is acute. The danger is imminent! Something must happen in the heart and soul of not only America but in the heart and soul of the church.

> *For this purpose the Son of God was manifested, that He might destroy the works of the devil (1 John 3:8).*

God's purpose in Christ was to annihilate the powers of darkness. Our purpose in Christ is to demonstrate that annihilation!

> *Cry loud, spare not, (Isaiah 58:1).*

To cry loud means to summon into court. Court is now in session. We are going to summon into court the evil one whom Peter said as a roaring lion walketh about, seeking whom he may devour. (1 Peter 5:8.) We are going to demand the presence of the one whom Paul called the prince of the power of the air and whom Jesus called the father of lies and the prince of this world. (Ephesians 2:2; John 8:44; John 12:31.)

And when we drag him into court we are going to bring him to the judgment seat of God. We are going to convict him, condemn him, bind him and cast him out!

Jesus said, *Behold, I give unto you power to tread on serpents and scorpions, and over all the power of the enemy; and nothing shall by any means hurt you (Luke 10:19).*

The authority to break the power of Satanic strongholds is available to you through Jesus Christ. You need to be set free. Your family needs to be set free. All around you a nation and a world need to be set free.

> *If the Son therefore shall make you free, ye shall be free indeed (John 8:36).*

Spiritual Warfare is Not a Game

Spiritual warfare is not a game, and the devil is not an innocent puppy. He is the master deceiver, thief, murderer and the force behind nearly all evil.

He is full of all kinds of cruelty, pain, curses and blight known to the human family.

He is the original instigator of separation between the Creator and His creation.

To survive his attacks, you must realize that the devil is a real enemy, hell-bent on destroying you. Determine to get serious about how to rebuke him and keep him from hindering your service to the Lord.

Satan hates every person who names the name of Christ. He especially hates the blood-bought, Holy Ghost-filled crowd that will not back down from him.

Now is the time for all the earth to break forth in praise and the mountains and hills in singing!

Everyone who names the name of Christ must release the power that is resident within them.

If we can receive a revelation of who Jesus is, we can take our place in the kingdom, and the gates of hell will not prevail against us (Matthew 16:18,19).

The only thing that the devil understands is for someone to come along with more power. There comes a time when you have to fight. No one likes to fight, but there comes a time when you must square your shoulders and join the battle. There comes a time when you must draw a line in the spiritual sand and say, "This is it. I am not going back, Devil."

Drawing the Line

Draw the line. This very day tell the devil to get out of your life and the lives of your family. Tell him you are not going back into bondage, and you are going all the way with God!

Chapter One

THE FACE
OF THE ENEMY

Who is the Devil?

We have all heard his names: Satan, Lucifer, the Dragon, the Serpent. We have all seen pictures of sinister looking devils running around in red pajamas with pitchforks. We have all heard the excuse given over and over — "It's not my fault. The devil made me do it."

Who is the devil, anyway?

Who is Like Unto Thee?
(Exodus 15:11)

First of all, know this: the devil is not God's equal. We have this idea in our heads that there is a great battle going on and the sides are evenly matched. We think of the forces of evil arrayed against the forces of good, battling it out tooth and nail for the future of the world. We hold our breath, wondering who is going to win.

I have good news for you. The sides are not evenly matched. They are not even close.

I was walking around the corridors of my church, World Harvest Church, one day, grumbling and complaining. I thought I was praying. The devil had been on my back all week.

Suddenly, God spoke to me in my spirit. When God speaks, you always remember exactly where you were. I can always mark the spot where He spoke to me.

He said, "Who is my equal?"

I stopped right in the middle of the hallway. There was no one else around, and I said, "What?"

And God repeated, "Who is my equal?"

The thought was so staggering to me, I had to sit down.

Immediately my mind ran to the Word of God that declares in Psalm 8:4-5, *What is man, that thou art mindful of him? and the son of man that thou visiteth him? For thou hast made him a little lower than the angels, and hast crowned him with glory and honour.*

I knew from my studies that the word here for "angels" is "Elohim," the Hebrew word for "God."

And God spoke to me from that verse. Men are not His equal. Governments are not His equal. Angels are not God's equal. They are not even our equal! As 1 Corinthians 6:3 says, we will someday judge these mighty beings.

And I began to realize what God was saying to me. Do Michael and Gabriel respond to the voice of the born again elect of God? When we speak forth God's Word, do angels minister on our behalf, hearkening to the voice of the redeemed of the Lord?

Yes! Psalm 103:20 tells us, *Bless the Lord, ye his angels, that excel in strength, that do his command-ments, hearkening unto the voice of his word.*

And I began to realize what God was telling me about the devil.

The Anointed Cherub

God is a triune God. He is the Father, the Son and the Holy Ghost. Man is a triune being, with a spirit, a soul and a body.

The Bible reveals an angelic creation with three major angels at its helm. One was Gabriel, the messenger angel. Another was Michael, the warrior angel. They had hosts of angelic beings under them in each of their positions ... and they still have them.

But there was a third angel.

Ezekiel 28:11-17 describes him:

Moreover the word of the Lord came unto me, saying, Son of man, take up a lamentation upon the king of Tyrus, and say unto him, Thus saith the Lord God; Thou sealest up the sum, full of wisdom, and perfect in beauty (v.11,12).

Sum means totality. There are three angels with high ranking listed in Scripture: Gabriel the messenger, Michael the warrior and Lucifer the light-bearer, son of the morning.

Thou hast been in Eden the garden of God; every precious stone was thy covering, the sardius, topaz, and the diamond, the beryl, the onyx, and the jasper, the sapphire, the emerald, and the carbuncle, and gold: the workmanship of thy tabrets and of thy pipes was prepared in thee in the day that thou wast created (Ezekiel 28:13).

Full of wisdom and perfect in beauty. He was the creation of God, the most beautiful and splendid of all the angelic creations. In his created form he was a living instrument. This jewel-encrusted angel was created with pipes in his being, and when Lucifer breathed, music would play through him. He was the leader of praise. When the heavenly hosts of God lifted up their voices and sang of the holiness and majesty of almighty God, Lucifer led them. He was in Eden, the garden of God.

Lucifer was given charge of the entire earth realm. He was commissioned to cause the earth to resound with praise before the throne of God.

The Bible does not describe Lucifer as a philosophical idea. He is not a symbol or a myth. Lucifer, in all his beauty, all his harmony, was created by God.

> *Thou art the anointed cherub that covereth;*
> *and I have set thee so: thou wast upon the*
> *holy mountain of God; thou hast walked up*
> *and down in the midst of the stones of fire*
> *(v.14).*

Lucifer was anointed by God! He walked in the presence of a holy God before His altar, directing celestial choirs as they glorified Him.

But something happened.

Pride Goeth Before Destruction

Proverbs 16:18 says, *Pride goeth before destruction, and an haughty spirit before a fall.* The first time in the history of the ages this ever happened was the day Lucifer set himself against God.

> *Thou wast perfect in thy ways from the day*
> *that thou wast created, till iniquity was*
> *found in thee (Ezekiel 28:15).*

Lucifer was created perfect. God was not the author of the iniquity that burned in Lucifer's breast and finally burst forth into rebellion.

> *Thine heart was lifted up because of thy beauty, thou hast corrupted thy wisdom by reason of thy brightness (v.17).*

Robed in the beauty God gave him, exhaling music beautiful beyond imagination, Lucifer decided being an anointed cherub upon the holy mountain was not enough. He wanted more.

> *For thou hast said in thine heart, I will ascend into heaven, I will exalt my throne above the stars of God: I will sit also upon the mount of the congregation, in the sides of the north: I will ascend above the heights of the clouds; I will be like the most High (Isaiah 14:13,14)*

Lucifer became puffed up in pride and said, "I will ... I will ... I will ... I will."

Ezekiel 28:16 adds, *By the multitude of thy merchandise they have filled the midst of thee with violence, and thou hast sinned.* Greed corrupted Lucifer — the lust for more. Perhaps he raised his fist into the air and declared, "I want! I will! I have a right!"

I Saw Satan Fall Like Lightning

The devil has already made his rebellious stand against the kingdom of God. It is over. I can imagine him presenting himself before the throne of the Almighty and saying, "I have come to tear your kingdom down."

I am certain God remained seated on His throne, and I can imagine Him saying to Michael, the warring angel, "Take care of Lucifer, the dog," ... and Michael cast him out of heaven. There was no mighty warfare with evenly matched armies struggling for control of heaven. God said it and it was done.

Fallen Angels

When Lucifer fell, he took the rebellious angels with him. They were once angelic beings who are now in a fallen state. Some of them are bound in chains of darkness in the deep, but not all of them.

> *God spared not the angels that sinned, but cast them down to hell, and delivered them into chains of darkness, to be reserved unto judgment (2 Peter 2:4).*

Jude 6 days, *And the angels which kept not their first estate, but left their own habitation, he hath reserved in everlasting chains under darkness unto the judgment of the great day.*

There is a lot of confusion concerning the origin of these demon spirits. There are teachers and preachers around who teach that demons are actually the disembodied spirits of a preadamic race. That is not what the Bible teaches. It teaches us they are fallen angels, no longer in their first estate. They serve their master, the devil.

Where are they Now?

The Bible teaches that there are three heavens. Paul

said, *I knew such a man (whether in the body, I cannot tell; or whether out of the body, I cannot tell: God knoweth;) such an one caught up to the third heaven (2 Corinthians 12:2).* If there is a third heaven, then there is a first and a second heaven.

The first heaven is the atmosphere of this earth. The second heaven is what the Bible refers to as the heavenlies. The third heaven cradles the throne of God, and some day we are going there.

But in the expanse of space between this earth's atmosphere and God's third heaven is what Genesis 1:8 calls *the firmament.* It is the only thing God created that He did not call good. Everything else was good, but God knew this area of space was to be the eventual dwelling place for Lucifer and his cohorts. The devil has access to the earth, but this is not his dwelling place. He dwells in the firmament. This is why Ephesians 2:2 calls him the *prince of the power of the air.*

He also has access to the third heaven. *For the accuser of our brethren is cast down, which accused them before our God day and night (Revelation 12:10).* And that is what the devil likes to do. In fact, it is the only thing he likes to do. The devil hates us, and he is bent on our destruction.

The Character of the Devil

John 12:31 calls him *the prince of this world.* The spirit of the world is a mirror of the devil's character. It can be summed up easily: selfishness, ambition, greed, fear, pride and rebellion. When you hear people say "I have a right," you should know where they are coming from. They are opposed to God. Ephesians 2:2 calls him *the prince of the power of the air, the spirit that now worketh in the children of disobedience.* (Ephesians 5:11 shows us disobedience brings darkness.) 2 Corinthians 6:14 exclaims, *What communion hath light with darkness?* None. They are opposites.

John 8:44 calls him *the father of lies.* Whatever he tells you, the opposite is true. He will tell you that you are going bankrupt, or you are going to get cancer and die. He will tell you your situation is hopeless, and God has turned His back on you. He sows seeds of fear and apprehension in your life. He lies about God.

This world is full of people who do not believe God exists ... or if they do believe it, they think He is a cruel and angry God waiting to catch them in their sin and strike them down with lightning bolts.

The devil has twisted the study of science and nature to persuade people that the Bible is not true. He has convinced an entire generation of people that wrong is right, evil is good, and sin is healthy.

2 Corinthians 4:4 calls him the *god of this world.* He is also the god of the world system. He was the god of the Babylonian system, the Egyptian system and the Persian system. He is the god of the current world order, the European Common Market and the financial institutions of the world.

2 Corinthians 11:14 calls him *an angel of light.* A better translation of this would be "enlightenment". It is no accident that the New Age was ushered in as "The Age of Aquarius" — the age of enlightenment. It is the age of the devil, when the god of this world blinds the minds of those who do not believe in Jesus Christ. The

Bible says *Satan is transformed (2 Corinthians 11:14)*, meaning that he is in disguise. The liar has dressed himself in the clothing of a messenger, spewing his lies and deceit over the earth.

What Does the Devil Want?

Make no mistake about it — the devil wants to destroy you.

Revelation 12:13-17 tells us:

And when the dragon saw that he was cast unto the earth, he persecuted the woman which brought forth the man child.

And to the woman were given two wings of a great eagle, that she might fly into the wilderness, into her place, where she is nourished for a time, and times, and half a time, from the face of the serpent.

And the serpent cast out of his mouth water as a flood after the woman, that he might cause her to be carried away of the flood.

And the earth helped the woman, and the earth opened her mouth, and swallowed up the flood which the dragon cast out of his mouth.

And the dragon was wroth with the woman, and went to make war with the remnant of her seed, which keep the commandments of God, and have the testimony of Jesus Christ.

The devil is at war. His goal is to torment and torture the creation of God. He wants to take as many people to hell with him as he can. He is bent on the destruction of anyone who could snatch victims out of his grip.

He wants to destroy Christians because they have the power to unmask his deceit and show others how to escape his deadly clutches. He hates the church. He wants to make the church ineffective to resist him and to set his captives free.

He is at odds with God, and his battlefield is your life. You belong to God but the devil wants to take you away from Him.

That is the source of all conflict in your life.

His purpose is to destroy you and everything you love ... everything that is good, holy and pure.

Jesus summed him up in John 10:10: *The thief cometh not, but for to steal, and to kill, and to destroy.*

That is Satan's purpose, and he is hell bent on doing it. He wants your joy, your family and your life. He wants to drag you into the eternal flames of hell. He is merciless.

What Can the Devil do to Me?

The devil may be the opposite of God, but he is not God's equal. He is not omnipotent. In fact, the devil has no real power.

Jesus said, *All power is given unto me in heaven and in earth (Matthew 28:18).*

The devil has no right to have any power. All he has are his abilities. The abilities he uses against the creation of God are deception and thievery. He lies and steals.

A thief does not have to be strong to steal. He can be scrawny and weak and still be the greatest thief the world has ever known. All he has to do is wait until there is no one home!

This is what the devil does. He preys on people who are "not home" spiritually. He stalks those who do not believe he is real, because he knows they will not be on guard against him. He lurks behind Christians who believe he is real — but leave themselves open to his oppression. He sets traps of temptation and deception.

2 Timothy 2:26 tells us backslidden Christians are in *the snare of the devil, who are taken captive by him at his will.*

He is subtle. He is a liar and a sower of doubt.

He is the enemy of all righteousness.

In Acts 13:10 Paul confronted Elymas, the sorcerer, who had tried to thwart the deputy's hearing and responding to the Gospel. Paul said, *O full of all subtilty and all mischief, thou child of the devil, thou enemy of all righteousness, wilt thou not cease to pervert the right ways of the Lord?*

That is exactly what the devil does. He perverts. He twists the truth, mixes it with lies and injects it with doubt.

He is our enemy.

Why is the World Getting Worse?

Have you noticed that the world is plagued by more evil than ever before? Have you noticed that people are more vulgar, vile and violent? Have you heard of the many wars breaking out all over the world and wondered why there are so many? Have you looked at the crime rates and wondered why they are rising so fast?

The devil has turned up the heat and is intensifying his attack.

Why? He knows the hour we are living in.

The curtain is going up on the final decade of destiny for the human family. The godlessness of the last days is upon us. The Word of God declares, *This know also: that in the last days perilous times shall come (2 Timothy 3:1).*

The devil is running out of time.

Revelation 12:12 says, *Woe to the inhabitants of the earth and of the sea! for the devil is come down unto you, having great wrath, because he knoweth that he hath but a short time.*

The devil's lease on this planet is almost up. He has had 6,000 years to run rampant over the face of the earth, and his time is now drawing to a close. The devil has pulled out all the stops in a final great outpouring of his wrath and hatred. He is frantic because the time of his destruction is approaching, and there is nothing he can do to stop it.

The Devil's Future

Let me show you just what is hanging over his head right now.

Revelation 20 describes the final end of the devil:

I saw an angel come down from heaven, having the key of the bottomless pit and a great chain in his hand. And he laid hold on the dragon, that old serpent, which is the Devil, and Satan, and bound him a thousand years. And cast him into the bottomless pit, and shut him up (vv.1-3).

After he has been bound for a thousand years, God will loose his chains and bring him out of the pit. The devil won't want to come out. He will cry and beg to stay in the bottomless pit.

Why? Because when he comes out he will be getting ready for his final incarceration, the one that will last forever.

Hell is real.

Mark 9:46 tells us hell is a place where *their worm dieth not, and the fire is not quenched*. It is the place where men gnaw their tongues for pain. It is an abyss of darkness into which men will be hurled for eternity, while their blood is shed to try to pay a price it can never pay.

Hell was not created for mankind. It was created for the devil and his fallen angels. Hell will be no less agonizing for Satan than for the souls he takes with him. Hell's gates yawn open before him, belching flames, smoke and eternal torment. He cannot escape.

But that is in the future. The devil is not in hell yet.

How are we to live victoriously until his final incarceration in Revelation 20? Today is where we are, and TODAY is when we must deal with him.

The Stronger Man

In Luke 11:20-22, Jesus said,

If I with the finger of God cast out devils, no doubt the kingdom of God is come upon you. When a strong man armed keepeth his palace, his goods are in peace: But when a stronger than he shall come upon him, and overcome him, he taketh from him all his armour wherein he trusted, and divideth his spoils.

The "strong man" is the devil and the goods in his palace have been stolen from us.

In his palace lies health, dignity and peace of mind stolen from us. He is hoarding our finances, our relationships, our opportunities and our blessings.

It is time for us to invade the strong man's palace.

But first we need to know the stronger man.

Chapter Two

CONQUEROR

Who is the Lord?

The Bible tells us in the book of Exodus that the children of Israel were taken into bondage by the Egyptians. Afflicted and abused, they cried out to God to rescue them from slavery. (Exodus 3:7.)

God heard the cry of His people and He raised up for them a deliverer, Moses: *Come now therefore, and I will send thee unto Pharaoh, that thou mayest bring forth my people the children of Israel out of Egypt (Exodus 3:10).*

Moses obeyed God's instructions. Along with his brother Aaron, he went before Pharaoh and boldly declared, *Thus saith the Lord God of Israel, Let my people go (Exodus 5:1).*

Pharaoh was not afraid. He was not even impressed. He did not apologize for holding Israel in bondage, and he answered Moses and Aaron with all the arrogance of absolute power:

Who is the Lord, that I should obey his voice to let Israel go? (Exodus 5:2)

Pharaoh found out who the Lord was. He found out through a plague that piled the land high with frogs. He found out when the dust of the land became lice that dug into the skin of both man and beast. (Exodus 8:1-19.) He found out when the Egyptians broke out in boils that festered and bled. (Exodus 9:8-12.) And he found out when the angel of death, passing over the homes of the children of Israel, brought to death the first born of every household, including Pharaoh's son. (Exodus 12.)

At their final moment of deliverance, God sent walls of water crashing down on the mighty armies of Pharaoh, while His people passed safely to dry ground. With signs and wonders, God destroyed the yoke of oppression crushing His children.

The devil is an oppressor. With his chains of sickness, violence and depression he holds people in bondage. With fetters of fear, deception and addiction he keeps people in his deadly grip.

Like Pharaoh, the devil seems to ask, "Who is the Lord that I should obey him?"

Stolen Dominion

God was the creator of the universe. With a word He separated light from darkness, formed the seas and dry ground, crafted the skies and flung the stars into space. He filled the universe with life, from lowly microbes to massive whales. He was over everything in creation and that He called good.

Then God decided to crown His creation with a living creature, unlike the others.

> *Let us make man in our image, after our likeness: and let them have dominion over the fish of the sea, and over the fowl of the air, and over the cattle, and over all the earth, and over every creeping thing that creepeth upon the earth (Genesis 1:26).*

God gave man dominion over the earth. This put a great responsibility on human beings. Humanity was given a lease on the planet with all authority to run it.

There was only one restriction:

> *Of the tree of the knowledge of good and*
> *evil, thou shalt not eat of it: for in the day*
> *that thou eatest thereof thou shalt surely die*
> *(Genesis 2:17).*

And with this one restriction, God gave man control over the earth.

But man lost it.

Actually, man gave it away. The devil, the great deceiver, slithered into the picture to sow diabolical seeds of doubt. "Hath God said?" he seemed to ask, and dangled before Adam and Eve the first documented temptation in history. *Ye shall not surely die,* he lied, *for God doth know that in the day ye eat thereof, then your eyes shall be opened, and ye shall be as gods, knowing good and evil (Genesis 3:4,5).*

Ye shall be as gods. Prideful ambition was Satan's downfall, and now it would be man's downfall. The moment Adam and Eve chose to doubt the words God spoke to them and willingly disobeyed His command, they committed high treason. In an instant they turned the rulership of the world over to Satan.

And when Satan took control, he brought devastation with him. The ground was cursed. (Genesis 3:17.) And Satan brought one more deadly consequence to man: death.

A Covenant God

A covenant is an eternal, unbreakable promise. God is a righteous God, and He will not break His covenant with man. He gave His word that man would have dominion over the earth. It was man's responsibility to keep dominion. When the devil stole it, dominion over the earth legally became his. For God to restore man to his rightful place and not change the rules, He had to work through a man.

Satan was immediately informed that he would be in control for only a limited time. God promised to raise up a deliverer for mankind.

> *I will put enmity between thee and the*
> *woman, and between thy seed and her seed;*
> *it shall bruise thy head, and thou shalt*
> *bruise his heel (Genesis 3:15).*

The Hebrew word translated *bruise* means "to crush." With these Words, God promised to send a human being, through the seed of woman, to defeat the power of Satan. Satan would be trampled under the feet of the deliverer and forced to yield control of the world to man.

The Righteous Seed

The devil had no idea exactly when the deliverer would come to wrest dominion back from his clutches. He only knew that the deliverer, the righteous seed, would descend from Eve. He looked suspiciously at her first two sons, Cain and Abel.

Satan could see that Abel, bringing the firstfruits of his flocks and offering a blood offering, was pleasing to the Lord. He could also see that Cain, who did not offer the first and best of his crops and brought no blood offering, was not pleasing to God.

Abel was the only possible candidate alive to be the righteous seed, so the devil enticed Cain to commit the world's first murder. (Genesis 4:8.)

But Abel was not the deliverer promised by God. Satan had failed to destroy the righteous seed.

The devil ran rampant over the world, bringing all manner of wickedness among men. Pagan religions grew up. Children were thrown into the fire as sacrifices to false gods. Sexual sin abounded. Lust, greed and violence spread until God decided to bring the great flood to cleanse the earth of mankind's wickedness.

But God preserved Noah and his family, keeping them safe in the ark while the flood destroyed the rest of mankind. Once again, Satan had failed to destroy the righteous seed, but now he had a clue. The deliverer would descend from Noah.

Over the years Satan kept right on corrupting. The newly populated earth again fell into sin and idolatry. In the midst of overwhelming evil, God spoke to a man named Abram, and called him to enter into an eternal covenant with God. (Genesis 17:2.)

Satan had a new clue. He followed the bloodline from Abraham, through Isaac, through Jacob, and through Jacob's sons. One day Jacob, about to die, pronounced blessings upon his children and revealed the line from which the deliverer would come:

> *The sceptre shall not depart from Judah, nor a lawgiver from between his feet ... and unto him shall the gathering of the people be (Genesis 49:10).*

Joseph and his brothers eventually died, and their descendants *increased abundantly, and multiplied, and waxed exceeding mighty; and the land was filled with them (Exodus 1:7).*

However, this land was Egypt. It was not long before Satan again moved against the righteous seed, enslaving the children of Israel and moving on the king of Egypt to decree that the male children were to be killed.

But God preserved Moses and, through him, led His people out of bondage. Satan, once again, failed to destroy the righteous seed.

Prophecy began to reveal more about who the coming Messiah would be. He would be a descendent of King David. The prophet Isaiah lifted up his voice and declared:

For unto us a child is born, unto us a son is given: and the government shall be upon his shoulder: and his name shall be called Wonderful, Counsellor, The mighty God, the everlasting Father, The Prince of Peace.

Of the increase of his government and peace there shall be no end, upon the throne of David, and upon his kingdom, to order it, and to establish it with judgment and with justice from henceforth even for ever (Isaiah 9:6,7).

The prophecy promised that the deliverer, the Messiah, would be the legal heir to the throne of David. Satan had convinced Judah to remain in idolatry. They did not heed the word of Jeremiah. Therefore, God pronounced judgment — exile.

Nebuchadrezzar, king of Babylon, marched through Jerusalem, doing whatever he desired.

In 586 B.C., Nebuchadrezzar, king of Babylon, and all his army besieged Jerusalem, destroying the walls and bringing destruction to the Temple. Zedekiah (the last king of Judah) ran for his life. The enemy pursued him, captured him, pronounced judgment and carried it out. This judgment included having Zedekiah's sons and nobles murdered, putting Zedekiah's eyes out, binding him with bronze shackles and taking him to Babylon. (Jeremiah 39:1-7.)

It appeared that no one would ever occupy the throne of David again. God had decreed it. The line of kingly succession had come to an end, and the Messiah had not come. Satan must have howled with laughter.

But God promised a seed would come! The enemy was working hard to prevent this seed from being conceived, *But when the fulness of the time was come, God sent forth his Son, made of a woman, made under the law (Galatians 4:4).*

One day Mary, a young virgin, found herself face-to-face with Gabriel, the messenger archangel who said,

> *Thou shalt conceive in thy womb, and bring forth a son ... He shall be great, and shall be called the Son of the Highest: and the Lord God shall give unto him the throne of his father David: And he shall reign over the house of Jacob for ever; and of his kingdom there shall be no end (Luke 1:31-33).*

Confronted with the dumbfounding news that she, a betrothed virgin, would be the mother of the Messiah, Mary said, *Be it unto me according to thy word (v.38).*

The righteous seed, which God protected from the beginning of mankind, was born in humble Bethlehem of Judea. He was named Jesus, which means salvation in Hebrew, *for He shall save His people from their sins (Matthew 1:21).*

His Legal Rights

The apostle Paul wrote that he was called by God to be separated unto the Gospel *concerning his Son Jesus Christ our Lord, which was made of the seed of David according to the flesh (Romans 1:3).*

The genealogy of Jesus could be traced through both sides of the family. Coming through the bloodline of David, Jesus had an indisputable claim to fulfill the prophecy of the Messiah.

He was born of a virgin. Without the virgin birth, there would not have been validity to the claim that Jesus of Nazareth was the Son of Man, a fulfillment of the Messianic title. (Daniel 7:13.)

Why was it important Jesus became a man? All dominion of this planet had been given to man. Satan hijacked it, but it was legally given to man. There was only one legal way to reclaim dominion over the earth, and it depended upon coming in through the right door.

Romans 5:12 says, *Wherefore, as by one man sin entered into the world, and death by sin; and so death passed upon all men, for that all have sinned.*

What Adam lost in the Garden of Eden, Jesus won back in the Garden of Gethsemane. *For as by one man's disobedience many were made sinners, so by the obedience of one shall many be made righteous (Romans 5:19).*

Jesus was the Son of Man, and he demonstrated His authority on earth over sin, sickness, demons, nature and poverty. He had entered earth's domain to regain lost rights. (Mark 2:10.)

Jesus entered through the door, which was Mary's womb.

A Specific Purpose

God anointed Jesus of Nazareth with the Holy Ghost and with power: who went about doing good, and healing all that were oppressed of the devil; for God was with him (Acts 10:38).

Jesus did not come merely to teach us about God. He did not come merely to perform miracles and healings for those He encountered during His lifetime. He did not come merely to set a good example for us.

Jesus came to the earth with a specific purpose.

God had something cosmically, eternally powerful to do on the face of the earth, and He was going to accomplish it through His Son.

1 John 3:8 tells us what that purpose was:

For this purpose the Son of God was manifested, that He might destroy the works of the devil.

Not only was Jesus manifested for that purpose, He was empowered for that purpose.

45

The word translated destroy in this verse is a powerful word. It means "to annihilate, to cause something to cease to be as though it had never existed."

What did Jesus come to annihilate? What did He come to destroy? He came to destroy the works of the devil.

Man has only one adversary in this world. It is not sickness. It is not slavery. It is not war, or crime, or poverty or death. It is the power that lurks behind all cruelty. It is the driving force behind all evil.

It is the devil — cast down from heaven, cursed in the Garden of Eden. Before the foundation of the world his destruction was pronounced.

And now Jesus came with one purpose — to destroy him.

Anointed

The Bible clearly tells us that Jesus was a man anointed. (Acts 10:38.) He was not the miracle-working Jesus of the Gospels because He was the Son of God. Jesus was who He was because of the anointing of God that rested on Him.

The day He presented Himself for baptism, Jesus *went up straightway out of the water: and, lo, the heavens were opened unto him, and he saw the Spirit of God descending like a dove, and lighting upon him (Matthew 3:16).*

Jesus Christ, the Anointed One, set out to destroy the power of the devil.

*And unclean spirits, when they saw him, fell
down before him, and cried, saying, Thou
art the Son of God (Mark 3:11).*

They cried in protest, trying to challenge his right
to rebuke them. But they failed, because He had the
right.

He cast out demon spirits wherever he went;
moreover, he delegated the same authority to his
followers. He sent them out to seek and destroy the
devil's oppression wherever they found it:

*Behold, I give unto you power to tread on
serpents and scorpions, and over all the
power of the enemy: and nothing shall by
any means hurt you (Luke 10:19).*

*And the seventy returned again with joy,
saying, Lord, even the devils are subject
unto us through thy name (v.17).*

The devils submitted. The devils obeyed. The
devils ceased their oppression and fled.

And then Jesus did something more.

Crucifixion

There was a crowd huddled outside Pilate's palace.
There was a grey haze hanging over Jerusalem. It was
the darkest day that would ever dawn on human infamy.

There was a figure slumped in Pilate's hall, barely
able to stand. He had been bound to the flogging post.
His back was laid open by the whip, and His flesh was
hanging around His legs. His face was so beaten He

could barely see through His swollen flesh. Roman soldiers spat upon His blood-soaked face, then took a crown of thorns and shoved it into His brow.

They cut Him loose from the flogging post only to kick and prod Him through the streets of Jerusalem, burdened with the staggering weight of His own cross. He dragged it as far as He could and fell. Simeon of Cyrene carried the Cross the rest of the way to a hill outside the city called Golgotha.

The soldiers laid His bloody body on that Cross. Without mercy they drove the nails deep into His flesh, and the blood spurted from His wounds. They nailed His feet and His hands to the rough wood and swung Him up between heaven and earth.

A Roman centurion watched from a distance. His heart had been hardened to the screams and wails of the criminals hung on Roman crosses. He had never cared before. But this time there was an eerie darkness, and he kept looking up at the man hanging between two thieves.

This man was not wailing. He was not screaming for His life. He had actually made the statement that no one took His life from Him, but He laid it down freely. And He had said, *I have power to lay it down, and I have power to take it up again (John 10:18).*

The centurion looked toward that Cross, and suddenly the ground began to move under his feet. He picked himself up and rushed toward the Cross, as the ground shook violently.

Suddenly, the condemned man lifted His head, and what the centurion heard was not a scream of despair or a whimper of pain. Jesus cried out, *It is finished! (John 19:30).*

It was a voice of triumph. It was a roar.

It was the roar of the Lion of the Tribe of Judah. It was the roar of the death slayer.

Resurrection

Satan laughed. He thought he had won. He looked upon the dead body of Jesus Christ laying in the tomb and believed he had at last destroyed the righteous seed of God.

Suddenly a light appeared at the end of the darkness. Jesus lifted the gates of damnation off their rusty hinges and walked up to the throne of the devil.

I believe Jesus must have grabbed the devil by the throat and cast him off his throne. I can see Him as He put one foot on the devil and the other on the crumbling empire of death and declared, I am Alpha. I am Omega. *I am the first and the last. I am he that liveth, and was dead; and ... I am alive for evermore... (Revelation 1:18).*

Mary came to the tomb on that third morning and found it occupied only by the angel who asked, *Why seek ye the living among the dead? (Luke 24:5).*

And the Son of Man was *declared to be the Son of God with power, according to the spirit of holiness, by the resurrection from the dead (Romans 1:4).*

God himself vetoed the crucifixion with the resurrection. Death was the last foe, and it was vanquished when Jesus arose victorious from the tomb. (1 Corinthians 15:55.)

The only thing that distinguishes Jesus from the central figure of every other religion on this planet is the resurrection.

Realize the provision that was made for you on the Cross. Just one drop of His precious blood is strong enough and powerful enough to deliver you from every situation that will ever cross your path by the hand of the devil. The provision was made on Calvary. The provision was fulfilled in an empty tomb.

The Conqueror

The Jesus of Revelation is the Jesus we serve today. Revelation 19:11-16 describes the risen, ascended, eternally victorious Son of God:

> *And I saw heaven opened, and behold a white horse; and he that sat upon him was called Faithful and True, and in righteousness he doth judge and make war.*

> *His eyes were as a flame of fire, and on his head were many crowns; and he had a name written, that no man knew, but he himself.*

> *And he was clothed with a vesture dipped in blood: and his name is called The Word of God.*

> *And the armies which were in heaven followed him upon white horses, clothed in fine linen, white and clean.*

*And out of his mouth goeth a sharp sword,
that with it he should smite the nations; and
he shall rule them with a rod of iron: and he
treadeth the winepress of the fierceness and
wrath of Almighty God.*

*And he hath on his vesture and on his thigh
a name written, KING OF KINGS, AND
LORD OF LORDS.*

What about the Devil?

*Then cometh the end, when he shall have
delivered up the kingdom to God, even the
Father; when he shall have put down all
rule and authority and power. For he must
reign, till he hath put all enemies under his
feet (1 Corinthians 15:24,25).*

Remember the promise God made to Adam and
Eve? He promised a deliverer who would crush the
devil's head under His feet.

Jesus is the deliverer. He has crushed the devil's
head and bought back man's dominion over the earth.

Jesus is now sitting at the Father's right hand:

*Far above all principality, and power, and
might, and dominion, and every name that is
named, not only in this world, but also in
that which is to come:*

*And hath put all things under his feet and
gave him to be the head over all things to
the church, Which is his body, the fullness of*

him that filleth all in all (Ephesians 1:21-23).

Together with Him we look forward to the devil's inescapable, inevitable end.

And the devil that deceived them was cast into the lake of fire and brimstone, where the beast and the false prophet are, and shall be tormented day and night for ever and ever (Revelation 20:10).

Jesus Christ, the Conqueror!

Chapter Three

MORE THAN CONQUERORS

God is a Good God

1 Peter 5:7 invites you to cast all your cares on God *for he careth for you.*

The first thing you must get settled in your heart is that God is a good God. He cares for you. Many don't understand this. God is full of blessing, mercy and abundance. He is the source of strength, health and vitality. He brings prosperity, joy, peace and security.

Every good gift and every perfect gift is from above, and cometh down from the Father of lights, with whom is no variableness, neither shadow of turning (James 1:17).

You can always be sure that the good things in your life have come from God. Not only that, you can always rely on His loving character to remain the same. God will not change. You will not come to Him one day and find Him in a good mood, and approach Him the next day and find Him angry and hostile. He is not a God of mercy on Monday and a God of unforgiveness on Tuesday. *I am the Lord, I change not (Malachi 3:6).*

Know the Word

The devil is a liar. He wants us to have a skewed view of God. We must never allow ourselves to believe anything about God that is different from what the Bible says.

Adam and Eve allowed themselves to doubt God's Word, and the world has suffered the consequences ever since. Every thorn and thistle, every poisonous plant and venomous viper should remind us that the devil is a liar. Listening to the voice of the father of lies only brings destruction.

Romans 4:20 gives us the example of Abraham, who *staggered not at the promise of God through unbelief; but was strong in faith, giving glory to God.*

The word "staggered" means "vacillated." People vacillate when they waver between opposite ideas or expectations. Abraham did not vacillate. He believed what God had to say about his situation. He did not go back and forth between two opposite expectations.

The battle with the devil will be won or lost in the arena of expectation. You will know what to expect if you know and believe what God has to say about your situation.

You cannot say one day that the devil has made you sick, then the next day decide God put that sickness on you to teach you a lesson, then the next day proclaim it was the devil again.

If you shift back and forth between two opinions, you are what the Bible calls "double-minded"; and the double-minded person will not receive from God. (James 1:8.)

Why not? Because the double-minded person lacks faith. My pastor, Dr. Lester Sumrall, describes faith as simply knowing God. When you know God, you are able to discern the difference between His work and the devil's work. You will be able to distinguish God's true Word from the devil's lies.

Until you get that into your spirit, you will constantly struggle with, "Is this from God or the devil?"

It is time you nailed it down.

Draw the Line

If you are going to live in absolute victory, you will have to draw the line. Take the pen of the Word of almighty God, dip it in the eternal blood of God's Son and draw a dividing line.

Where? The same place Jesus drew the line:

The thief cometh not, but for to steal, and to kill, and to destroy: I am come that they might have life, and that they might have it more abundantly (John 10:10).

Most anything in your life that is killing, stealing or destroying can be attributed to the devil, not to God.

Sickness does not come from God.

Depression does not come from God.

Financial trouble does not come from God.

Most of the destructive forces in your life come from the devil.

You don't serve the devil. You don't belong to the devil. The devil has no right in your life, because Jesus came to set you free.

We are at War

Romans 8:35 asks a question:

Who shall separate us from the love of Christ? Shall tribulation, or distress, or persecution, or famine, or nakedness, or peril, or sword?

Romans 8:37 answers the question:

Nay, in all these things we are more than conquerors through him that loved us.

Notice that little two-letter word "in." God did not say "outside" of these things. He said "in" these things. In tribulation ... in persecution ... in peril.

There is a war going on.

When Jesus came out of the tomb and defeated the devil, I'm sure the devil did not just crawl off in the corner like a whipped puppy. He bared his teeth and growled. He is determined to make life miserable for those who love God and drag as many into hell with him as he possibly can.

The devil has targeted you. His wagons are circled around your house. He has stolen from you. He has taken your peace, afflicted your family, stirred up strife, interfered with your finances and stolen everything he could lay his hands on.

The Bible says that in the midst of all this, you are more than a conqueror. But to be a conqueror, you must first enter the battle. You cannot be a conqueror until you fight the enemy and win.

Greater Works Shall You Do

Remember, I told you all the devil understands is someone who has authority and uses it.

Jesus has the power of God. He entered the world legally and went forward in His human body, armed with the power of God to *destroy the works of the devil (1 John 3:8)*.

Because of this, born again believers have authority also.

You are the legal heir of the dominion God originally gave man and that Jesus took back for us at Calvary. You entered this world through the right door. You are a human being. And you have something else. You have the same power Jesus had.

Jesus said, *He that believeth on me, the works that I do shall he do also; and greater works than these shall he do; because I go unto my Father (John 14:12)*.

Jesus declared in Matthew 16:18, *I will build my church, and the gates of hell shall not prevail against it.*

You are part of that church. The gates of hell shall not prevail against you, because of the power of God inside you.

The Temple of the Holy Ghost

There will come a time when the miraculous will become explosive beyond measure. Paul wrote, *Know ye not that ye are the temple of God, and that the Spirit of God dwelleth in you? (1 Corinthians 3:16).*

He was not asking a rhetorical question. The temple he spoke of is not just a symbol, or a figure of speech. It is your body. The Holy Spirit of God resides within you.

When God brought the children of Israel out of bondage, He wanted to dwell among them. He told Moses to build a tabernacle. In the tabernacle was a room called the Holy of Holies, and the ark of the covenant was kept in that room. The ark was also called the ark of the Presence, because the very presence of God dwelt there.

Inside the ark were the stone tablets containing the Ten Commandments, God's Word to His people. Where His Word resides, God resides, and wherever His Word is, that is where He will manifest Himself.

When Jesus came, God gave us a new covenant. He said, *I will put my laws into their mind, and write them in their hearts (Hebrews 8:10).*

If God writes His Word on our hearts, and our bodies are the temple of the Holy Ghost, what does that mean for us today?

It means the same presence of God that was inside the Holy of Holies is now inside you!

Treasure in Earthen Vessels

2 Corinthians 4:7 says, *But we have this treasure in earthen vessels, that the excellency of the power may*

be of God, and not of us.

We are the earthen vessels, containers made of dust and clay. The treasure inside us is the very presence of God. His presence is in you. That is the treasure we have in these earthen vessels.

Paul wrote that he had been made a minister to fulfill the Word of God, including the mystery of the ages that was now being revealed to those who received Jesus as Savior. That mystery is: *Christ in you, the hope of glory (Colossians 1:27).*

The Holy Spirit indwells you for a purpose.

Why does the Holy Spirit need to be inside you?

There are no angels going into the world preaching. The Holy Spirit Himself does not preach. Jesus told US to go into all the earth and preach the Gospel.

James 4:7 says, *Submit yourselves therefore to God. Resist the devil and he will flee from you.* Many skip over the first half of that verse. That is why the devil is still able to torment them.

In order to make the devil flee from you, you must first submit to God. You must allow His Holy Spirit to dwell in you. You must receive the power and authority that only Jesus Christ can give you. Then you can resist the devil.

Paul also wrote, *I am crucified with Christ: nevertheless I live; yet not I, but Christ liveth in me... (Galatians 2:20).* This is true for all of us who receive Jesus as Savior. Jesus lives in us.

Jesus never changes. He is *the same yesterday, today and forever (Hebrews 13:8).*

He cast out devils while He was living on the earth, and He casts out devils today.

Greater is He that is in You

When you command the devil, it is not you commanding him at all. It is the Spirit of God that resides within you that commands the devil to go.

Alone, you are no match for the devil.

But you are not alone.

We are not in a physical wrestling match with the devil. He is not a natural being. The battle is between the Holy Ghost in you and the devil's minions coming against you.

Remember, the sides in this conflict are not evenly matched.

The Bible says, *Greater is He that is in you, than he that is in the world (1 John 4:4).*

If a priest went into the Holy of Holies and there was any sin found in him, he would die. Sin was the work of the devil, and sin could not stand in the presence of the glory of God.

So if you bring the works of the devil into contact with the presence of the glory of God in you — they will go! Away with discouragement. Away with burdens. Away with sickness. Away with defeat.

Know Your Authority

The devil is a liar. He wants to deceive you into thinking God is far from you instead of living in you. He wants you to believe God's Word does not mean what it says. He wants you to believe that while the Word of God may be true for some people, it is not true for you. It is in Satan's best interest to keep you in the dark about the power that resides in you.

1 Peter 5:8 says, *Your adversary the devil, as a roaring lion, walketh about, seeking whom he may devour.*

Notice it does not say he is a lion. It says he is "as" a roaring lion. He only pretends to have the power of the lion.

He is a creature with a big mouth. He is roaming to and fro, with no earthly idea where he is going. He is seeking whom he may devour.

Whom can he devour? Those who do not know the Word. Those who do not know that he has been defeated. Those who do not live in relationship with Jesus Christ and do not have power and authority over all devils.

Because we do not know the authority that is ours, we have let the devil run roughshod over our lives. I think it is time we gave the devil permission to do one thing only, and that is to stare at the bottom of our feet.

Are you tired of your family being lost? Are you weary of being the tail and not the head? Are you fed up with that sickness, that depression, that cold, gnawing fear? You should be tired of every manifestation of the devil in your body and in your life.

I believe it is time we squared our shoulders like a T-rail and told the devil we know he is defeated and has no authority, or right, or portion in our life. It is time we cast him out.

Just before Jesus ascended into heaven, He instructed His followers to go into all the world, preaching the Gospel. *And these signs shall follow them that believe; In my name shall they cast out devils (Mark 16:17).*

God has never amended His Word. He did not say, "Some of my followers will cast out devils, for a short time, and then the power will disappear." He said, *In my name shall they cast out devils.* That means you will cast out devils.

Resist the Devil

God will never back down from the devil. He knows our enemy. God knows every trick, every tactic, every evil scheme Satan uses. When the Holy Spirit lives in you, you have all the ammunition you need to ward off the enemy's attacks and force him to retreat.

It is time to get the works of hell under our feet! It is time to resist the devil and watch him flee from us.

James 4:7 says, *Resist the devil, and he will flee from you.*

Strong's Concordance defines *resist* as "oppose" or "withstand."

And he will *flee* from you. The word *flee* also has several layers of meaning.

Newman defines flee, "to run away, disappear, vanish."[7] Arndt translated this verse as, "seek safety in flight."[8] Harold K. Moulton defines it, "to set in opposition; stand out against."[9]

My favorite translation is from the Greek Expositor's New Testament which reads: "He will be vanquished. He will run from you disgraced."

Stand Up to the Enemy

Jesus said, *Behold I give you power to tread on serpents and scorpions, and over all the power of the enemy: and nothing shall by any means hurt you (Luke 10:19).*

It is time to stand up to the enemy.

How long, fathers? How long, mothers? How long, husbands, wives, sisters and brothers are you going to put up with the devil? How long will you allow him to walk into your home, spread discouragement, cloud the air with depression, and slap your loved ones with sickness?

It is time to draw the line in the spiritual sand and command the devil to get back on his side, in Jesus' name.

The time for diplomacy is over. There will be no deals, no discussions.

It is time to confront the oppressor and say, "I will not ask, I will not beg. I will not tell you what a good idea it might be for you to let go of what belongs to me. I do not come in the name of men. I am coming against you in the name of the Lord of Hosts, the Lord of Glory, the great I AM."

We may be down, but we are not out! We have the Word of God inside us, and we are ready to use our holy arsenal and drive the devil out.

You are the victor, not the victim. You are the overcomer, not the overcome. You have authority over all the works of the devil.

We are more than conquerors.

You are more than a conqueror.

You are more than a conqueror, because the Conqueror lives in you.

Chapter Four

EXPOSING THE DEEDS
OF DARKNESS

Exposing the Deeds of Darkness

We are seeing an explosion of demonic activity in these last days. Hordes of devils have been unleashed upon America in an effort to deceive, seduce, addict, cripple and destroy the people God desires to save.

You may have experienced their attacks in your life or in the lives of those you love. You may live in a neighborhood caught in the grip of devils. Your workplace, your city and your nation have been targeted for destruction.

As we go forth into battle in the name of Jesus, we will encounter many kinds of demonic influence and oppression. Some of the most common influences fall into five categories: spirits of degradation, spirits of infirmity, spirits of deception, spirits of divination, and what I call "spirits of demise."

Spirits of Demise

The word "demise" means death. John 8:44 says of the devil, *He was a murderer from the beginning*. He is still a murderer today. We can see the manifestation of these spirits of demise on the rise in suicide, murder and abortion.

The Spirit of Suicide

A preacher recently asked his congregation, "How many of you have been contemplating taking your life?"

Hundreds of people raised their hands. Hundreds!

Suicide is the third leading cause of death among teenagers in this nation.[10] There are teenagers sitting in our churches who have lost all hope, who feel as if no one cares about them, who feel as if there is no way out. The rate of teenage suicides increased approximately 400 percent between 1960 and 1990![11]

It begins with hopelessness.

A pastor friend of mine once said, "Hopelessness is when you don't believe tomorrow can be any different than today."

Two high school honor students from one of Long Island's finest high schools laid down in front of a rushing train in what police called a "double suicide." They were described by friends as normal teenagers from stable, loving families.[12]

Only weeks before summer vacation, when kids are supposed to be excited and looking forward to swimming and having fun, a San Ramon boy shot himself in the head, becoming the third thirteen-year-old boy at his school to kill himself in recent months. Nobody knew why; students and teachers thought he was happy, with every reason to live.[13]

Another boy, only eleven years old, took a .38-caliber semi-automatic handgun from his father's bedroom and brought it to school in his backpack. He shot himself in the head at the entrance to his Los Angeles school.[14]

What is happening in our homes and in our nation — when even our teenagers have no hope for tomorrow?

The devil is crafty and he is cunning, but he is not very brave. When he comes after us, he seeks the wounded, the weak and the weary. He preys on those who cannot defend themselves. Countless souls have been trapped by his diabolical lies of hopelessness until they see suicide as the only way out.

Euthanasia is the next rung on his ladder. "After all," many seem to think, "what do we need the old people for? They are no longer useful." There is a phrase that has been going around for years now, "a useless eater." This is a phrase right out of hell! It proclaims the idea that any living human being is expendable.

A Michigan circuit judge recently ruled that terminally ill patients have a right to commit suicide.[15] A book about ways to take your own life made the New York Times Best Seller List in 1991. There is a vast audience of hopeless souls in our nation who are listening and responding to the wicked spiritual forces who encourage suicide.

The number one season for suicides is spring. Why not the holidays? Why not winter, when the world is cold and bleak? A survey of people who had survived suicide attempts revealed the reason: in the spring, they were reminded of life. Everything was beginning new, and they had no hope of a new beginning. They had no life, and everything around them made them realize how dead inside they really were.

The Spirit of Murder

I gave an altar call recently for people who were having dreams of loss, dreams of abandonment, emptiness and loneliness, dreams of blood and death. The altar area was jammed with people.

By the time the average child in America is 16 years old, he has seen 200,000 acts of violence on television, including 33,000 murders.[16]

Not long ago in Kentucky, a high school honor student only 17 years old, walked into his Trigonometry class and pulled out a gun. He laid it on the desk and calmly announced to his teacher, "I've had a really bad day, I just killed my family." The police went to his $300,000 home and found his father, mother and 2 sisters shot to death.[17]

A bad day? There's a devil loose!

Jim Huberty left Ohio for California and began reading the satanic bible and attending seances. Eyewitnesses reported that objects would move around in his home on their own. Dressers would move out into the middle of the room, and the drawers would open by themselves. Windows would open of their own accord.

One day he put on army fatigues, took an automatic weapon in each hand and said, "I'm going to hunt men." He walked into a fast food restaurant and began firing. Twenty-one people lay dead in the aftermath, drowning in their own blood, before he finally shot himself.[18]

A teenager or child in this nation dies from a gunshot wound every two hours. Murder is the third leading cause of death among children ages five to fourteen![19]

It used to be that to prosecute for murder the court had to have proof of motive, means and opportunity.

Now murderers do not even have motives. A drive-by shooting claims a stranger's life. A man goes berserk in a commuter train and opens fire. A woman is strangled at work by a man who walked in the door, just "to see if he could do it."

The Spirit of Abortion

There was a time when you could say the word "abortion" to a congregation of believers and their blood would run cold. Now it barely gets a response. We have become accustomed to it.

We have become desensitized to the fact that little bodies are pulled apart, wrenched from their mothers' wombs and placed in garbage bags. In 1990 there were approximately 1.6 million abortions. Today nearly 1 in 4 pregnancies ends in abortion.[20] We are using it as birth control.

The numbers are staggering. Six million aborted babies would have been teenagers today. Eleven million would have been in elementary school, and one million of them would have been three-year-olds playing around our feet.[21] But they are dead, and America no longer weeps.

We worship the pagan gods of desire and lust, then sacrifice human lives on the altar of our own lust!

I opened the yellow pages of the telephone directory the other day. On page two I noticed an advertisement, nestled among pictures of roses, butterflies and trees. It had a list of the "possible after effects of abortion." Right after the list of horrifying medical damages, including sterility, I found the following: "trauma, depression, spontaneous crying, anguish, loss, nightmares, psychological scarring, suicidal tendencies."[22]

Has anyone ever stopped to think about the mothers of those aborted babies? The secular press wants you to believe that abortion solved their problems. Abortion rights groups want you to believe those mothers merely exercised their right to reproductive choice. Editorial cartoonists want you to see them as the persecuted victims of hateful pro-life demonstrators.

Who will tell you about the mothers who search frantically through closets in the middle of the night, trying to find a crying baby? They cannot silence its cry from their ears, and they weep as they search for the infant that was butchered while still inside their bodies. Who will tell you about their remorse, sorrow and regret? The proponents of godless legislation, who want to include abortion on demand in a national health care program will not.

In 1993 our president signed into law a bill that allows the dismembered bodies of these murdered babies to be used in fetal tissue research.[23] The irony is the research is supposed to find ways to save lives.

On Planned Parenthood's "Dollar a Day" program, it offers $1 to participating teenagers for each day they don't get pregnant. Of course, the girls can be sexually active and still get the money, as long as they use birth control devices. The program cost $657 per girl in 1993.

One of the teenagers in the program said, "Some of the girls have been in the group since they were twelve." An adult coordinator added, "No one was sexually active then. And now, everyone, of course, is."[24]

Spirits of Degradation

Spirits of degradation are sweeping over America. Attacking in the area of sexuality, the devils pervert the beautiful experience God intended sex to be. By wresting it out of the God-ordained context of marriage, these devils have infused the nation with immorality. In direct defiance of God's Word they have promoted homosexuality. With sinister cunning, they prey on women and children by arousing lust through pornography.

The Spirit of Immorality

Hosea 5:4 calls it the *spirit of whoredoms*. We see this foul spirit manifested today in adultery, prostitution and rape.

The national conscience can be summed up in the words of U.S. Surgeon General, Jocelyn Elders, who said, "I tell every girl that when she goes out on a date, put a condom in her purse." [25] Sex is an assumption.

A physics teacher in the Bronx High School of Science is a leader and promoter of NAMBLA — the North American Man/Boy Love Association.[26] Their goal is to make it legal for men to have sex with minors, including little boys.

Two brothers, one seven years old and one nine, have just recently been accused of raping a five-year-old girl in Illinois. They were too young to even be arrested. [27]

A Lakewood, California gang called the "Spur

Posse" has violated and exploited hundreds of girls as young as ten years old. One of the members commented, "They pass out condoms, teach sex education, and pregnancy-this and pregnancy-that. But they don't teach any rules." [28]

They don't teach any rules because they don't know any rules! The Surgeon General of the United States has said "We taught them [teens] what to do in the front seat. Now it's time to teach them what to do in the back seat."[29] It's the spirit of whoredoms.

The Spirit of Homosexuality

The Ohio State University is the largest single campus in the United States,[30] and estimates that 5,400 homosexuals are among its 52,200 students.[31]

This is not an acceptable, alternative lifestyle. This is a demon spirit. It traps men. It traps women. It is a force against nature and a force against God.

While I was growing up, I do not remember my pastor ever using the word homosexual. If he had, it would have caused no small stir. Now we are supposed to call them gay. I have never met a happy homosexual in my life, but we call them gay. The truth is, they are not gay. They are miserable, devil-oppressed individuals.

The gay rights groups protest that they are merely living an alternative lifestyle and they were born that way. They promote the lie that ten percent of America's population is homosexual. We are not supposed to think anything is amiss when men are having sex with men and women with other women.

Homosexual characters appear on television programs more and more frequently, always in positive roles. Homosexual activists have tried to represent their demands as civil rights issues, calling for "justice" as they demand homosexual marriages, spousal insurance coverage, and even the right to adopt children!

On September 19, 1993, members of the Hamilton Square Baptist Church in San Francisco were attending their Sunday evening service when they were attacked viciously by the gay activist groups ACT-UP and Queer Nation.

The church was surrounded by more than 100 rioters who screamed obscenities and roughed up parishioners who were attempting to attend the service. When the protesters saw boys and girls inside the church, they shouted, "We want your children, give us your children!"

A nine-year-old boy was crying hysterically, "They're after me! It's me they want!" The pastor begged for police support but his request was denied. He was told, "You must understand, this is San Francisco." [32]

No arrests were made.

The University Congregational Church, one of Seattle's largest churches (1,250 members), which is often described as one of the most liberal Protestant denominations, is one of the few to sanction homosexual ordinations. They recently hired two gay pastors, when the congregation voted 473 to 143 to hire them. Only 15 members quit. Another pastor of a 3,600 member Christian Church preached against the couple's hiring, stating, "It's the most obnoxious thing in the world. It's anti-Biblical. It's anti-decency." The United Church of Christ has 25 to 50 openly gay ministers, and Unitarian Universalists have about 100.[33]

Confused and overwhelmed by sex in any case, and now bombarded by talk of homosexuality in the press, in school sex education classes and in entertainment, lots of kids are calling themselves "gay" to be trendy or rebellious. According to The Washington Post, bisexuality and homosexuality have become the "in" thing among the high school and junior high school set. [34]

A pastor friend of mine told the heartbreaking story of a man who had lived in a homosexual lifestyle for many years. He came to a service dying of AIDS and gave his life to Christ, but soon went back into the gay lifestyle.

This pastor was later driving down the street and saw that same man with lesions all over his body, doubled over in pain, holding his hand out, begging. He was not begging for money. He was not begging for relief from the pain. He was begging for a man to come and fornicate with him.

Dr. Lester Sumrall has seen the demon spirit of homosexuality and says, "The demon of homosexuality is so ugly, so grotesque, that all the other demons hide their eyes from it because they don't want to see it. And when they see it, they regurgitate because it's so sickening."

The Spirit of Pornography

I was in the airport recently to pick up a guest speaker. I had not been in that airport for two years because I hate to go there. At eight o'clock in the morning I have seen men go into those gift shops— men who just kissed their wives and hugged their babies— and open magazines with pornographic photographs and stare as if they were animals in heat.

All you have to do is turn on CBS, NBC or ABC to see the kind of trash that used to be banned from television.

Serial killer Ted Bundy, before his execution, gave an interview in which he admitted the role pornography had played in twisting his life. His warning is going unheeded. Sales are skyrocketing.

I watched on television Ted Bundy's interview with Dr. James Dobson, given the night before he was executed. Ted Bundy, who demonically murdered, raped and ravaged, was a handsome young man with a brilliant mind, raised in a Christian home.

Sitting handcuffed in his jail cell, he told Dr. Dobson that he shuddered to think of the kind of people who are walking around in society. He told of how, as a young boy, he found discarded pornography and detective magazines along the back roads. He began to feed his fantasies on them, and they helped mold and shape his violent behavior. [35]

That was twenty years ago. He did not have X-rated movies broadcast over cable television. There were no video stores peddling pornographic films. He could not find sex shops on every corner as we can now. He could not walk into a convenience store and see stacks of pornography. What must it be like today? How many people like Ted Bundy are out there?

What kind of a generation are we living in when men feed themselves on pornographic filth? We cannot allow our children to go out to play unsupervised in safety, lest someone like Ted Bundy, who spent his life feeding at the pig trough of pornography, abducts them.

We often hear the stories of parents called by the police to come and identify the remains of their children. We have heard of those who were so mutilated they had to be identified by their dental records. The victims are boys as well as girls.

We have the most advanced printing presses and computer typesetting ever available to publish the Word of God, yet billions of dollars are spent publishing child pornography.

Janet Reno, the Attorney General of this nation, released her statement on child pornography saying, "It is not pornography unless there is actual visible penetration of the child."[36]

Spirits of Infirmity

No one could argue that we are getting sicker and sicker. The devil has poured out wasting disease over the face of the earth. In our medically progressive society, cancer, heart disease and stroke are snuffing out hundreds of thousands of lives every year. Health care reform is such a hotly debated issue because of the enormous sums of money we pour into doctors, hospitals, drugs and therapies. The devil is ravaging our bodies and taking our lives at a pace that almost defies description.

Antibiotic-resistant strains of bacteria are causing the deaths of people who would have recovered just a few years ago. These "superbugs" emerge from the battle with antibiotics stronger than they were before.

Doctors are beginning to prescribe multiple medicines to treat the same condition, in the hope that at least one of the kinds they use will kill the bacteria.

Viruses, untouchable by antibiotics, are becoming more virulent than ever. Every year brings a new strain of influenza, deadlier than the last.

In May of 1994, there were 369,000 reported cases of full-blown AIDS in the United States. The Center for Disease Control will give no estimates of those infected by the HIV virus, but who have not progressed to the AIDS diagnosis yet — because the numbers are staggering. They predict that by the year 2,000 everyone in the United States will personally know someone who is infected.[37]

Jesus said there are spirits of infirmity. We have all known people afflicted by these devils. Just as soon as they get free from one sickness they get another. Three months after they recover from an illness, it comes back.

Spirits of Terror and Fear

Wicked spirits torment the mind. The Bible speaks of a *spirit of terror and the spirit of fear (Isaiah 54:14; 2 Timothy 1:7).*

The entertainment industry promotes terror. The news media promotes fear. It seems as though the bloodier and more heinous they can make it, the more people want to buy it, look at it, read about it and know about it.

All over America today we see people bound by fear. We see them tormented in their minds. They are afraid of the dark. They are afraid of failure. They are in bondage to fear of sickness and disease. They are in bondage to fear concerning their finances.

The secular counselors can diagnose all kinds of "phobias," which are defined as "morbid dreads." Some of these are as crippling as the fear of walking outside your own front door. Hypochondriacs, those who fear being ill, waste their lives going from doctor to doctor, trying to discover nonexistent diseases.

Spirits of Deception

The Bible calls the devil a liar, and the father of lies. His insidious lies are being spread all over the nation and the world, enticing people to fall away from the Word of God and become entangled in false doctrines.

Seducing Spirits

The Bible says, *Some shall depart from the faith, giving heed to seducing spirits, and doctrines of devils; speaking lies in hypocrisy; having their conscience seared with a hot iron (1 Timothy 4:1,2).*

Seducing spirits will attempt to draw you away from the truth of God. James 1:14 says, *But every man is tempted when he is drawn away of his own lust, and enticed.*

"Drawn away" is a hunting term. It means to be lured, or to be seduced away from safety into the snare of the hunter. One use of the word enticed is a fishing term, meaning to "take the bait." When we take the bait, the hook is set in our jaw and we are drawn into the snare of the devil.

Today we have over 100,000 Black Muslims in America preaching separation and death.[38] The devil is sowing hatred, murder and fear among us, trying to undo the work of great men like Martin Luther King, Jr.

The Jehovah's Witness' publication, <u>Watchtower</u>, is now printed in 106 languages; and 17.8 million copies are distributed each month.[39] Scientology has seen explosive growth, with over 6 million members in 35 countries.[40] Mormonism now boasts a worldwide membership of 6.5 million, an estimated income of $1.3 billion each year and assets of $8 billion.[41]

These cults are filled with former Christians. They have listened to seducing spirits and allowed themselves to be drawn away.

Spirits of Bondage

There are 25 percent of Americans who have lung disease directly associated with smoking. The Surgeon General plainly states on placards all over America that we are killing ourselves with tobacco. We spend $48 billion annually on cigarettes alone, while the cost of health care for smoking-related diseases averages $262 annually for every person living in America ... not every smoker — every man, woman and child.[42]

The National Institute on Alcohol Abuse and Alcoholism reports that 15.1 million people in the United States are either alcoholics or alcohol abusers, and that 107,800 deaths yearly are attributed to alcohol alone.[43]

As 118 million watched the 1989 Super Bowl game, they witnessed a very subtle contradiction. During a break in the play, Oral Herschiser, of the Los Angeles Dodgers, stood before a camera and begged kids to say "no" to drugs. He said, "Losers use and abuse." Yet the very next commercial featured another sports celebrity holding up his favorite beer and saying, "It doesn't get any better than this."[44]

Alcoholism has ravaged families and torn lives apart. In my spirit I hear the cry of a little girl who sobs quietly in her bed at night. She gently nurses the black and blue bruise on her cheek because daddy came home drunk.

In the next house lies a lonely little boy whose daddy has not been home for days because he has disappeared in the neighborhood of crack houses.

In another, a woman waits in fear and trembling, because her husband has discovered cocaine gives him a bigger thrill than marijuana. But cocaine brings on rage, which he releases in violent abuse.

Down the street a drug deal has gone sour, resulting in a spray of bullets that will leave two teenagers dead and one paralyzed.

The Antichrist Spirit

There is an antichrist spirit loosed in the earth. It has been around for many, many years. Paul said it was already at work in the earth. We see it on the increase today.

It is a spirit of lawlessness. The crime rate in the United States in 1994 is higher than any other industrialized nation, and the fastest growing segment of the criminal population is our nation's children![45]

The FBI reports that the nearly quadrupling in juvenile arrests has involved not only the "disadvantaged minority youth in urban areas," but "all races, all social classes and lifestyles." [46]

While our population has increased only 41 percent since 1960, violent crimes have increased more than 500 percent and total crimes over 300 percent. The U.S. Department of Justice has predicted that 8 out of every 10 Americans will be a victim of violent crime at least once in their lives. [47]

Spirits of Divination

The New Age movement is not new at all — it is one of the oldest lies on the face of the earth. It is Eastern mysticism dressed up in Western clothing. There are 100,000 New Age bookstores now operating in America, with 30 new ones opening every month.[48] That is an average of 1 every day.

Shirley MacLaine recently boasted that the Bible was a mystical book that taught plainly the victories of reincarnation, and claimed that her personal spirit guide is none other than the Virgin Mary.[49]   While seeking to trap new converts into belief in the deadening cycle of reincarnation, the New Age movement has transformed man's fundamental question from "Who am I?" to "Who was I?"

A poll conducted by the University of Chicago revealed that 67 percent of the public claims to have psychic experiences.[50]   Over 50 million Americans believe their destinies are determined by the movements of celestial bodies. [51]   Another recent study indicated that "60 percent of Americans consider reincarnation a reasonable probability." [52]

New Age educators are working to win acceptance of the "Impressions" curriculum for first through sixth grades in all 50 states. [53]   A third grade reader contains an innocent-looking illustration entitled, "Shut the windows, bolt the doors."   It shows floating objects, and the manual instructs the teacher to have all the children write and chant spells to make objects in the room float. [54]

Familiar Spirits

The National Spiritualistic Association of Churches, the oldest and largest of spiritualistic bodies, was formed in 1893. Combined with 20 other Spiritualist denominations, church officials estimate there are more than one-half million adherents. [55]

A survey by the National Opinion Research Council shows that nearly 50 percent of American adults believe they have been in contact with someone who has died. [56] They have actually been in touch with familiar spirits, masquerading as people who have died.

Mission SOAR (Set Objectives, Achieve Results) is a program which was piloted in the Los Angeles school district to help reduce gang violence and build self-esteem. Students are taught to communicate with the dead and receive guidance from their spiritual guides on how to plan their future lives. [57]

Mission SOAR very closely parallels the techniques found in <u>Beyond Hypnosis: A Program for Developing Your Psychic and Healing Powers</u>.

Ouija boards, tarot cards, palm-reading, automatic writing, trance mediums and channeling are methods familiar spirits use to communicate. People who claim to "hear voices" should not be dismissed as crazy — they may be hearing from familiar spirits.

Spirits of Devils (Witchcraft)

Because some witches are reluctant to announce their pagan affiliations, estimates of those involved in organized witchcraft in the United States today range from 100,000 to 600,000. [58] You do not have to go to South America or Botswana to find a witch. You need only go downtown.

In October, 1993 a group of witches and warlocks went down to the statehouse in Columbus, Ohio. There was a rally scheduled for the Klu Klux Klan that provoked much argument in the city, so the witches decided to help by "cleansing the atmosphere."

Have you ever heard the phrase "white witchcraft?" It is astonishing how many practitioners of witchcraft actually believe their powers are beneficial and good.

Dr. Sumrall, described how over forty years ago in the mountains of Central America, he met a witch doctor. That witch doctor was a strange character. He took a bullfrog and poured a mixture of blood and wine into its mouth. He then closed its mouth and began to dance around, worshiping demon powers. He asked them to come into him, possess him and give him great power.

If you think that was only going on forty years ago in Central America, you may be surprised. It is going on right now in Miami. It is happening today in Chicago. It happens in Los Angeles. It is going on all over America. People are begging for demon power to possess their bodies and give them power, and the spirits of darkness are entering through those open, welcoming doors.

Voodoo thrives in South Carolina, Texas, Mississippi, Louisiana and Florida. Law enforcement officials say that animal sacrifice rituals in the Miami area are so common the river's clean-up boat picks up an average of 100 carcasses a week! [59]

Santeria, a form of voodoo, practices the slaughtering of animals as an offering of blood to appease their gods. One Santeros (priest) said, "The saints have to be fed, and blood sacrifice is one of the ways you feed them."[60]

Fear Not, for I am with Thee

There is a way which seemeth right unto a man, but the end thereof are the ways of death (Proverbs 14:12).

America today is in a wasteland of bondage. The chains that bind people's bodies, hearts and minds do not only affect those outside the church, but also those inside.

Many are bound to the occult and mysticism. Many are bound to New Age philosophy. Others are bound to the torments of relentless fear.

Many are bound by the addictions of drugs and alcohol. Many are bound by perversions, lesbianism and homosexuality. Many are bound by lawlessness, violence and hatred. Many do not know what kind of spirit they are bound to.

Many do not even know they are bound.

But they are in bondage, and they need to be free.

You need to be free.

When the enemy shall come in like a flood, the Spirit of the Lord shall lift up a standard against him (Isaiah 59:19).

The power of God is available to deliver anyone who needs to be set free.

No matter what the devil has put on you, God is strong enough to take it off. No matter what the devil has stolen from you, God is strong enough to take it back.

Behold the battle-scarred Lord of Glory. He stands before you, a shepherd's rod in His right hand — stained with the blood of your defeated enemy. Now look down and see the roaring adversary, laying mortally wounded at His feet.

This is the victorious Lord who says, *Fear thou not; for I am with thee (Isaiah 41:10).* There is a power living in you that has trampled the devil under His feet. (Romans 16:20.) His strength is in you, His anointing is upon you, and nothing is impossible to you, for all things are possible to him who believes.

Chapter Five

BREAKING THE BONDS
OF DARKNESS

Fetter Free

I am amazed by the designs of God. I am continually awed by the plans God has devised for us. Nothing happens by accident. He made each one of us and appointed this time for us to live. We have been given our bodies, handed back our dominion and sent forth with absolute authority to accomplish His work in the world.

Our authority is not limited to this world. We have authority in the same world God inhabits, the realm of the spirit. We have authority in the regions of the heavenlies where lurk the powers of darkness.

We need never again put up with the unfruitful works of darkness. We need never again submit ourselves to sickness, infirmity or any bondage the devil and his minions would bring against us.

When you fight the devil, you are fighting the good fight of faith.

Faith in what?

Faith to believe that what God has spoken is true.

God said Jesus was manifested to annihilate the works of the devil, so it is true. Jesus said we would do greater works than He did on earth, so it is true. (John 14:12.)

And Jesus said we would have the power to tread upon serpents, so it is true. (Luke 10:19.)

Drive Out the Intruders

Remember, between the earth where we dwell and the third heaven where God dwells is the firmament. It is here that the fallen angels dwell. (Ephesians 2:2.) That is where they belong, until they are cast into hell at the end of time.

When God gave man dominion over the earth, He *put him into the garden of Eden to dress it and keep it (Genesis 2:15)*. The word "keep" (shamar, Hebrew) means to guard, or be a night watchman. It is the same word used for the cherubim that is to guard the tree of life from intruders. (Genesis 3:24.) God literally meant to drive out all intruders. The only intruder in that garden was Satan, and that was the downfall of man — not that Satan was there, but that man did not drive him out.

We must also drive out the intruders and possess our God-given ground. "Possess" means to take dominion, but it means even more than that — it means to drive out and make poor the previous tenants.

The domain we are going into, the realm of the spirit, is saturated with demonic power. There is a domain in your own life, the spirit realm of your existence. It is your responsibility to take dominion in that realm and drive out the previous tenants.

All of us have a specific area in the realm of the spirit for which we are responsible. The spiritual atmosphere of your life — and dominion over it — has been given to you and no one else. You have more authority in your life than all the preachers in America put together.

In your area of dominion, there are probably some intruders. You may be aware of them right now. You may be suffering from the bites and stings of those serpents and scorpions.

It is time to drive them out, but driving them out is only part of what you need to do. The word "possess" also means to occupy (by driving out previous tenants and possessing in their place).[61]

Possessing the Land

The previous tenants are not poor yet. They have in their possession those things that rightfully belong to us. They have everything they have stolen from us.

Christians do most of their warfare defensively. They do not come into the spirit realm to invade — they come to try to get something off them the devil has already put on. They come seeking to regain something the devil has already stolen from them.

We need to dwell continually in the realm of the spirit. We must no longer settle for running in and out of that arena of conflict after disaster has already struck us. We cannot wait for the devil to show up and manifest his destructive work before we decide to invade.

You are not fighting a defensive war. Jesus said, *He that believeth on me, the works that I do shall he do also (John 14:12).* He did not say we should look at the diabolical works of the devil in our lives and ask, "God, would you please take care of this?" or "God, why aren't you doing something about this mess?"

God wants to prepare the way before you in the realm of the spirit so you can live in victory, with the devil firmly pinned under your feet.

The Bible calls the devil in 2 Thessalonians 2:8 the "wicked." The Greek word literally means against or in opposition to the law. Some translations say "the lawless one." You are the law enforcement agent of your life. You have been authorized to take your handcuffs and go into the spirit realm to apprehend him!

Jesus promised, *Whatsoever thou shalt bind on earth shall be bound in heaven... (Matthew 16:19).*

We have work to do. And we have greater works to do.

Have Faith in His Name

In Mark 16:17, Jesus said, *And these signs shall follow them that believe; In my name shall they cast out devils.* The semi-colon was inserted in that text much later. It does not belong there. What Jesus said was, *These signs shall follow them that believe in my name.*

The followers of Jesus came back from their assignments rejoicing, saying, *Lord, even the devils are subject unto us through thy name (Luke 10:17)*. Like those followers, you also must have faith in His name when you go to battle against the devil. When you are called by His name the devils will fear and tremble.

In Acts 3, Peter and John healed a crippled man at the Gate Beautiful. But they were soon surrounded by accusers who demanded an answer to the question, *By what power, or by what name, have ye done this? (Acts 4:7).*

They replied, *By the name of Jesus Christ of Nazareth, whom ye crucified, whom God raised from the dead, even by him doth this man stand here before you whole (Acts 4:10).*

And their accusers commanded them *not to speak at all nor teach in the name of Jesus (Acts 4:18).* They did not command them to leave town. They did not tell them they could not speak or teach. Peter and John were commanded not to use the name of Jesus.

There is power in that name.

Have faith in that name!

The Sons of Sceva

Acts 19:13-16 tells us what happens to people who try to use the authority of Jesus without having faith in His name.

The seven sons of the Jewish exorcist Sceva confronted a man who was possessed by an evil spirit:

We adjure you by Jesus whom Paul preacheth ... And the evil spirit answered and said, Jesus I know, and Paul I know; but who are ye? And the man in whom the evil spirit was leaped on them, and over- came them, and prevailed against them, so that they fled out of that house naked and wounded.

The sons of Sceva failed because they were not living in relationship with Jesus, therefore they were not called by His name. There was no indwelling Spirit of God inside them commanding that devil, and they confronted it without the authority that only comes from God.

I love what T.L. Osborne says that when you know who God is, what God has, and what God can do, then you find out who you are, what you have and what you can do. Then it is exposed what your enemy has and what he can do. And when you know the first two, the answer to the last one is — nothing. Absolutely nothing.

That is why you must be born again before you attempt to go into the spirit realm to fight. You have to have the indwelling Spirit of God inside you. When you stand up to the powers of darkness, you must come in the name you know and are called by and have the authority to use — the name of Jesus.

The Holy Spirit will take you right into the realm of the spirit and make the introduction. I like to imagine that He says, "Hey, dogs. Listen here. Principalities and powers, listen. This is a child of God who has been washed—"

The demonic hordes will cringe and shrink back, crying, "Not those next words! Please, not those next words!"

The Holy Spirit continues, "—washed in the blood of the Lamb. Whatever he says to you, the Father and the blood are backing him up!"

The Blood of Jesus

You need to learn how to plead the blood of Jesus.

The blood is for more than eternal salvation. The blood is for your protection. Jesus shed sinless blood that the devil could not cross. When we plead the blood of Jesus we can do it in authority, with boldness and with confidence, knowing there are not enough devils in existence to cross that line. If they all joined hands and pushed together, they still could not cross that line.

My property has a blood line. My house has a blood line. My family has a blood line. Your dominion in the spirit realm has a blood line, and you have to draw it.

In Exodus 12, God told the children of Israel to take the blood of lambs and paint the lintel of their doors with it, so the angel of death could not cross that blood to reach those inside.

We can apply the blood of Jesus in the realm of the spirit. We can dip our brushes in the eternal, everlasting blood of the Lamb of God and paint it on the doorposts of our hearts. That blood will proclaim, "No entry, devil. We give you no place. You cannot come in!"

And the devil cannot cross the line.

Pleading the Blood

"Jesus, I thank you for the precious blood you shed for me at Calvary. I thank you for the protection your blood provides for me today. The devil cannot penetrate the blood of Jesus. Right now I plead the blood of Jesus over my life. I plead the blood of Jesus over my body, mind and spirit. I give them all to you. I come into agreement with the Word of God, and I reject every thought that does not agree. I renounce every lie of the devil, and I refuse to listen to any more of his lies. I reject all the works of the devil, and I raise up a covering of prayer over my life. In Jesus' name I pray, amen."

Confession: the First Step to Freedom

The first step to freedom is confession.

The Greek word translated "confess" is homologeo. It means to say the same thing.

When you confess what God's Word says about you, you are speaking in agreement with God's Word. You are agreeing that what God has said is true. You are saying that what God is showing you about your life is true. You are declaring that sin is sin because God said so. You are declaring that you are in the condition God says you are in. You are proclaiming that you need what God says you need.

A preacher's wife once said she wanted to get away from all distractions and get into the presence of God. She went alone to a remote cabin and began to pray, "Oh, God, I want to see you. God, I want to feel you. God, I want to know you. God, I want to sense your touch."

She prayed for about twenty minutes, and suddenly God began to show her sins and inconsistencies in her life. She continued praying, and God kept showing her more and more what was wrong in her life.

Finally she became exasperated and said, "I am leaving this cabin if something doesn't happen. I came all the way up here to see you and all I have done is see me!"

And God said, "After you have seen yourself enough to take care of what is inside you, then you can see me."

We cannot hear or feel God if we are not pure in heart.

You may have gone where you should not have gone, seen what you should not have seen, and done what you should not have done. You may have allowed doubt and unbelief to creep into your mind.

The average Christian is so cold hearted toward God and so full of the world, there is no place left into which the Holy Spirit can rush in satisfying fullness. We are too full of our will, our wants, our ways and our plans.

> *Search me, O God, and know my heart: try me, and know my thoughts: And see if there be any wicked way in me, and lead me in the way everlasting (Psalm 139:23,24).*

David was saying, "There are things in me I may not even know I am holding against you; and unless you help me see them, I cannot see them. But if you will help me, God, I will see them."

There is a purpose for confession. 1 John 1:9 says,

> *If we confess our sins, he is faithful and just to forgive us our sins, and to cleanse us from all unrighteousness.*

Confess your sin and receive His forgiveness. Let Him cleanse you from unrighteousness. Then and only then will you be qualified to stand against the devil in His authority and name.

Repentance: the Second Step to Freedom

The second step to breaking the bonds of darkness is to repent of your sin.

The Greek word for "repent" is metanoeo, and it means to change one's mind. It means to change your direction. It does not mean to change your direction slightly. It is a 180 degree turn. It is a total about face.

But you cannot turn from something unless you turn toward something.

God never delivers you only "from." He delivers you "from" and "to."

When He delivered the children of Israel, He delivered them from Egyptian bondage and to the Promised Land.

When we repent, we are leaving something behind and going on to something else.

Repentance is not apologizing. In fact, God despises apologies. Apologies are excuses, and God is not interested in excuses.

How can you know whether you have repented or apologized? By how many times you have done it. If you have repented four or five times for the same sin, you have not repented, because you have not turned away from it.

If someone drinks on Friday and repents on Sunday; then drinks Monday and repents on Wednesday; then drinks Friday and repents on Saturday — he is not repenting. He may be turning from, but he is not turning to.

Repentance is not saying, "Okay, I did this and I am sorry." Repentance is "I have godly sorrow over what I have done, not because I was caught or because I am afraid of going to hell, but because my relationship with my Father is hindered."

Let me give you an illustration. Before you is a dish of dog food and a plate with a T-bone steak. God points to the dog food and says, "That is what you have been eating." Then He points to the steak and asks you to make a choice. This is why the Bible says, *the goodness* — not the meanness — *of God leadeth [us] to repentance (Romans 2:4).*

Conviction — Our Friend

Conviction is a good thing. It is like feeling pain in your body. The pain is not your enemy; it is only an indication that one exists. Without pain you could walk down a beach, step on a broken bottle, and continue walking while your blood drained out. You would eventually collapse and die, because you had no warning. Pain warns us that something is wrong.

That is what conviction is. Do not confuse it with condemnation and rise up against it, saying "Don't condemn me." Recognize the nudging of the Holy Spirit that tells you something is wrong and needs to be changed.

Acts 3:19 says, *Repent ye therefore, and be converted, that your sins may be blotted out, when the times of refreshing shall come from the presence of the Lord.*

God is saying, "If you repent, I will send times of refreshing. And after I refresh you, I will restore you. I will restore your peace. I will restore your authority. I will restore your courage. I will restore your power."

Repentance is not penance. You do not have to do anything to make God forgive you. You do not have to pray for hours. You do not have to cry. You do not have to kneel until your feet are numb. All you have to do is obey the Word of God.

When you take one step toward God, He will take three steps toward you.

The Prayer of Salvation

If you have never given your life to Jesus and entered into a personal relationship with Him, you can do it right now.

Pray these words out loud now, and receive His saving, delivering grace:

"Heavenly Father, I confess to you that I was born a sinner, and I have committed sins. Today you have sent your Word to deliver me. I repent of my sin, and I ask you to forgive me and wash me in your blood. I accept you now as my personal Savior.

"I humble myself in your sight and acknowledge your Lordship. You are God and I am not. I acknowledge my desperate need for you. I acknowledge that in your love for me you have called me, redeemed me and destined me for victory.

"I thank you for your overwhelming mercy and the sacrifice of your only Son. I thank you, Jesus, for going to the Cross for me. You took my sins, my burdens and my sorrows into your own body as you laid down your life for me.

"Satan, I renounce you. I am coming out of your prison. You cannot hold me. Jesus has made me free.

"Thank you, Lord, for seeking me and finding me. Thank you for dying for me and setting me free. I commit my life to you, and I will serve you forever. In Jesus' name, amen."

The Prayer of Recommitment

Perhaps you have prayed before to receive Jesus as your Savior, but you know you have not been living your life for Him. If this is true, you can recommit your life to Him now by praying this simple prayer:

"Lord Jesus, I come to you now to recommit my life to you. I confess that I have fallen away from the things of God. I repent of my sins and I turn away from them now.

"Forgive me for allowing the spirit of the world to attach itself to me. Just as Paul shook off the viper into the fire, I now shake off the world, in the name of Jesus. I reject the world.

"I accept your blood. I kneel at your Cross, and I receive your forgiveness. I will live for you as you show me how, in Jesus' name, amen."

A New Creature

Therefore if any man be in Christ, he is a new creature: old things are passed away; behold, all things are become new (2 Corinthians 5:17).

Are you in Christ? If you are, that means the devil is on the other side of the line. All things on your side of the line are of God.

Let us see what has happened now that you are in Christ.

Greater is He that is in you, than he that is in the world (1 John 4:4).

By the power of the Holy Spirit, you have the awesome authority to tell the devil what to do.

Now then we are ambassadors for Christ, as though God did beseech you by us: we pray you in Christ's stead, be ye reconciled to God (2 Corinthians 5:20).

You now speak in Christ's place.

To whom ye forgive any thing, I forgive also: for if I forgave any thing, to whom I forgave it, for your sakes forgave I it in the person of Christ (2 Corinthians 2:10).

You have authority to minister in Christ's place.

In the sight of God speak we in Christ (2 Corinthians 2:17).

Are you allowing these truths to flow into your spirit?

You are just about ready to make the devil get back on his side of the line.

Rebuke: the Third Step to Freedom

Rebuke means "Stop it!"

Rebuke means "Enough is enough!"

The Bible tells the story of Peter's mother-in-law, who was taken with a great fever. (Luke 4:38,39.) Jesus came to her home and "stood over her."

God is standing over you today. He is standing between you and the forces of darkness that would try to attack you.

God is standing between you and sickness, pain, malady and malfunction.

And, He is not just standing there quietly. When Jesus stood over her, He *rebuked the fever; and it left her: and immediately she arose and ministered unto them (Luke 4:39).*

When Jesus rebuked the fever, it means he told the devil in no uncertain terms, "Stop it!"

I was in a meeting with Brother Norvel Hayes in 1979. I was a life-long Baptist boy, and I had no experience with spiritual warfare.

I had just left the meeting and was walking down

the hallway, when suddenly a woman came around the corner and lunged at me.

She was dirty and had a sickening body odor, but there was another odor around her. It was an odor of death.

A blue, milky film covered her eyes to the point I could not even see her pupils.

As she leaped through the air at me, I saw the knife.

"Lucifer is god," she shrieked.

One of Brother Hayes' assistants was with me at the time. He tried to grab her, but she threw him off as if he weighed nothing at all.

She screamed again, "Lucifer is god!"

Suddenly a supernatural peace came over me. I was not nervous or upset. She came at me again with the knife, and I said, "Stop!"

I did not even add, "in Jesus' name." That was understood. I was in Him and He was in me. I was living, walking and breathing in Jesus' name.

She came to an abrupt stop. It was as if someone had grabbed her arm, but no one was even near her. She could not move.

Then she started to regurgitate fluid. I again said, "Stop it. I command you, stop it."

She stopped.

I said, "You lying devil, in the name of Jesus Christ of Nazareth, I know my authority over you, and I command you right now, by the authority of God's Word and the Holy Ghost of God and by the blood of the Lamb, come out of her."

No one taught me how to do that. I watched Brother Hayes and Dr. Sumrall exorcise demons, but I had never done it before.

She cried, "Satan is god!"

I responded, "Satan was defeated by the blood of Jesus at Calvary. I have commanded you once, and I have commanded you twice, and I am not going to command you again to come out of her!"

This time I perceived that something went forth from me. Suddenly I felt as if I could hardly stand up. Every ounce of spiritual strength shot out of me.

Suddenly that milky color left her eyes and her pupils appeared. She stood upright and said, "Where am I?"

I told her where she was, and she asked, "How did I get here?"

I did not know how she got there, but I knew how she was going home — free!

Rebuking the Devil

If Satan has a hold on you, you do not have to put up with his bondage another moment. Pray this prayer to break his chains now:

109

"Satan, by the authority of the Word of God and by the blood of the Lamb, I rebuke you. Stop it. I command you to go from me now. Take your hands off my life. Loose your hold on my mind, my heart and my body. I agree with the truth of the Word of God. According to Matthew 16:19, whatever I bind on earth is bound in heaven. I bind you and cast you out."

Resist: the Fourth Step to Freedom

The Greek word for "resist" is antistateo, which means to stand against or oppose. It also means "to put pressure on." When you are standing is the only time there is pressure under your feet.

When you rebuke the devil, he stands still. When you resist the devil, you step on his head, crushing him to stillness.

In the book of Joshua, God told the army of the children of Israel that He would destroy their enemies if they would devote their cities to Him. The same Hebrew word for destroy and devote, cherem, is translated "flat nose" (Leviticus 21:18). When Joshua was destroying the cities, he was literally giving the enemy a flat nose.

I believe God used this Hebrew pun to say, "Punch your enemies in the nose, take back what was originally intended for you and reclaim your land!"

As a child of God you have the authority to punch the devil in the nose and take back your stolen property ... without suffering any casualties.

*Resist the devil and he will flee from you
(James 4:7).*

How do you resist him? In word and deed.

You have to speak out the Word of God and you have to take action to successfully resist the devil.

The Word did not say "Get saved and the devil will flee." It does not say "Go to church and the devil will flee." In fact, when you draw close to God, you let the devil know you are a force to be reckoned with ... and he is going to come against you. To make him flee, you must resist him.

To resist means to constantly set yourself against the devil and be hostile toward him. When was the last time you were hostile toward the devil? When was the last time you talked to that devil of doubt? When was the last time you stood up to the spirit of unbelief, or criticism, or the spirit of fear?

Declare, "I do not put up with the devil!" the next time unbelief comes into your heart. Shout it the next time fear grips your mind.

I traveled to West Virginia to preach in a church a few years ago, but by the time I arrived, my voice was gone. I could not say a word. I arrived at three o'clock, and I was scheduled to preach at seven o'clock that evening. I only had four hours to get my voice back.

That afternoon I took my Bible — and I read to the devil. I still did not have a voice. He had to read my lips. But I told him that I was resisting him.

I said, "According to Isaiah 53:5, by the stripes of

Jesus I am healed. My voice is strong. I am anointed to preach the Gospel of Christ. The devil has tried to bind my voice so I cannot preach the Word of God and set the captives free, but I rejoice that the devil is defeated. According to James 4:7, I resist the devil. I give him no place in my life. I thank God I will deliver the Word of God with fullness into the hearts of the people."

All the time I was mouthing these words, no sound was coming out of my mouth.

When the pastor of the church came to pick me up at six o'clock, I still had no voice. He said, "You cannot preach tonight." But I assured him with many gestures that I could most definitely preach.

The moment I stepped behind the pulpit, with a Bible in one hand and a microphone in the other, God met me. I preached over two hours and was stronger when I finished than when I started.

I resisted the devil in both word and deed. You resist him when you smile, when you shout and when you clap your hands.

You resist him when you pray. You resist him when you speak in tongues. You are meant to resist the devil, trampling in triumph over serpents and scorpions every moment of your life.

Temptation, when repelled and constantly kept at a distance, ceases to exist. I do not know what the devil has tried to do in your life, but I know this. If you will resist him, he will flee from you.

Fill yourself with the presence of God. Give the devil no place. Resist him and watch him run in terror.

Refill: the Fifth Step to Freedom

*When the unclean spirit is gone out of a
man, he walketh through dry places, seeking
rest; and finding none, he saith, I will return
unto my house whence I came out. And
when he cometh, he findeth it swept and
garnished. Then goeth he, and taketh to
him seven other spirits more wicked than
himself; and they enter in, and dwell there:
and the last state of that man is worse than
the first (Luke 11:24-26).*

When evil spirits are cast out, they are on the
lookout for a place to rest. If they do not find a place to
dwell, they will try to return to the same house. Jesus
said the house must be clean. It must also be full so
there is no room for the spirit to re-enter.

You must be filled to overflowing with the Holy
Ghost.

Ephesians 4:27 says, *Neither give place to the devil.*
The word for place in this verse is topos, which means
"a position of opportunity."

Give the devil no position of opportunity. Keep
the door shut. More than that, keep something flowing
out under the door, through the cracks and through the
keyhole. Keep the presence of God flowing continually.

When the devil shows up at your house and you
are full of the Holy Spirit, he will find a spiritual sign
that says, "No Vacancy."

He will not be able to gain a place of opportunity
in your mind, because your mind is renewed in the Word

of God. You are thinking on whatsoever things are true, honest, just, pure, lovely and of a good report (Philippians 4:8). You are thinking about God's authority and ability. There will be no room for the devil to get in.

Drink in the Word of God. Ephesians 5:17 says, *Be filled with the Spirit.* In this passage in the original Greek language, it is present tense. It means to be continually filled. It is not a one time event. It is a crisis event with abiding results. A fresh baptism, as commanded in the Greek, means it is absolutely necessary for the success of a believer.

Prayers for Prevailing Power

Be careful for nothing; but in every thing by prayer and supplication with thanksgiving let your requests be made known unto God (Philippians 4:6).

Prayer is approaching God. Prayer is coming from where you are to where God is. Prayer is making your petitions known to God. Prayer is communing with, conversing with, asking and receiving from God.

Hebrews 4:16 says, *Let us therefore come boldly unto the throne of grace, that we may obtain mercy, and find grace to help in time of need.*

If you have a time of need in your life right now, I want you to know you can approach the throne of God and find grace there to help you. God has an inexhaustible supply of grace. And we come to that throne of endless grace in the name of Jesus.

114

Ephesians 1:21 says the name of Jesus is far above *every name that is named, not only in this world, but also in that which is to come.*

The name of Jesus is above alcoholism, drug addiction and violence. The name of Jesus is more powerful than financial pressure, depression and thoughts of suicide. The name of Jesus is stronger than rebellion, confusion and lawlessness. It is the name above cancer. It is the name above fear. It is the name above all the works of the devil.

Think of your child on crack cocaine. Think of the divorce papers that are about to be filed. Think of the pain in your body, or your loneliness or the alcoholism that is consuming someone you love.

There is power for every situation in the name of Jesus.

There is power to heal your body, save the lost, take control of your finances and overcome every obstacle the devil may put in your way.

However, prayer is not just a formula or a method to get what you want. It is direct communication with the sovereign God of the universe. It depends entirely upon your being in personal relationship with Him. You have absolutely no power in and of yourself. It is the Spirit of God dwelling inside you that has power. You must get into the spirit to get involved in the flow of God.

Paul expressed this when he said, *I am crucified with Christ: nevertheless I live; yet not I, but Christ liveth in me (Galatians 2:20).*

Mountain, Be Thou Removed

*For verily I say unto you, that whosoever
shall say unto this mountain, Be thou
removed, and be thou cast into the sea; and
shall not doubt in his heart, but shall
believe that those things which he saith
shall come to pass; he shall have
whatsoever he saith. Therefore I say unto
you, what things soever ye desire, when ye
pray, believe that ye receive them, and ye
shall have them (Mark 11:23,24).*

If you have committed your life to God and
received Jesus as your personal Savior, you will be able
to proclaim as Paul did, *Christ liveth in me*. (Gal. 2:20.)
Then, when you speak to the mountain in your life, you
will be speaking at God's prompting. It will be God's
will for the mountain to be removed.

The Will of God

What is the will of God?

The will of God is no secret. We need only turn to
the Word of God to find out what His will is:

*I am come that they might have life, and
that they might have it more abundantly
(John 10:10).*

The will of God is life-giving. Everything in your
life that steals, kills and destroys is not the will of God.
Nothing that steals, kills and destroys is the will of God.

Disease is not the will of God. Financial ruin is
not the will of God. God does not desire that we live

our lives in despair and defeat. He takes no pleasure when we experience abuse. He does not want anyone to fall prey to the deception of the devil and die unsaved.

It is God's will that the works of the devil be destroyed!

Prevailing Prayers

Stealing the Word: "Satan, I know you come immediately to steal the Word. I bind you. I serve notice on you, Satan: you are rebuked. Stop it. That is enough. You will not steal one more word, not one more revelation, not one more insight about the character of God and the power of His indwelling Spirit."

Suicide: "You foul spirit of death, I rebuke you and command you to stop your influence. I lift up before the throne of God every one who is tormented by thoughts of hopelessness and suicide. I pour forth your spirit into those situations. I rebuke the spirit of depression now, in Jesus' name."

Murder: "I come against the spirits of anger and violence. I rebuke the spirit of hatred. I bind the spirit of murder, and I command you to stop now. Come out, in the name of Jesus."

Immorality: "By the blood of Jesus and His authority, I speak to the spirits of immorality, homosexuality and pornography. I bind you according to Matthew 18:18 and I cut off your power. In Jesus' name, I silence your voices and command you to go."

Disease: "I speak to every illness, infection and imperfection. Lying spirit of disease, you cannot stand in the presence of Jesus Christ. You cannot stand in the presence of the blood of the Lamb. I plead that blood now.

"I command cancer cells to die. I command destructive viruses and bacteria to die. I command the spirit of life to come in. I adjure all sickness and malady to obey the Word of God and go, in Jesus' name."

Fear: "Tormenting spirit of fear, I call you to account. It is written in 2 Timothy 1:7, *God hath not given us the spirit of fear; but of power, and of love, and of a sound mind.* You have no place here. I adjure you, by the blood of Jesus, to loose your hold and come out."

Deception: "Spirits of deception and seducing spirits, I command you to silence your lying voices. You have been defeated by Jesus Christ, the Truth, and you cannot remain in His presence. I command you to go now."

Addiction: "By the authority of the Word of God and the blood of the Lamb, I set the boundary on drug and alcohol addiction. I rebuke that alcoholic devil, in the name of Jesus. I rebuke that spirit of addiction, in the name of Jesus. I command you right now, loose your hold."

Rebellion: "Spirit of rebellion, I stand in covenant blood with Jesus Christ who has defeated you. I adjure you by His authority and command you to loose your hold on every mind and body. You are bound and rendered helpless. Obey the Word of God and depart."

Divination: "Spirits of divination and witchcraft, I bind your deceitful and abominable works, in the name of Jesus. I come against you by the power of the Cross and tell you to leave now, in His name."

Salvation: "Satan, I rebuke your attempts to blind the lost to the truth of the Gospel of Jesus Christ. In the name of Jesus, I command you to take your fingers out of their ears and your hands from over their eyes. Cease your lying tongue and stop your influence over their minds now, in Jesus' name."

Finances: "Devil, I command you to get under my feet. In the name of Jesus, take your hands off my property. Stop hindering me in my finances. Stop stealing from me. Put back what you have taken from me, in Jesus' name."

Relationships: "I come against conflict and the spirit of disunity, in the name of Jesus. I rebuke your efforts to disrupt my relationships. I refuse to listen to your lies about my family members, my friends and acquaintances, my neighbors and co-workers, my pastor and the members of my church. I will not submit to your influence any longer. Go from me now, in Jesus' name."

Prayer of Thanksgiving

"Father, I thank you that you have revealed your life-giving nature to me through your Word. I praise you that you never change and that your Word is forever settled in heaven. Thank you that I am what it says I am. I have what it says I have. I can do what it says I can do.

"Thank you, Lord, that it reveals to me who you

are, who the devil is and who I am. Thank you that your Word speaks to every conflict in my life. Thank you for your indwelling Spirit, that gives me the power and authority to stand against the adversary and all devils.

"Heavenly Father, I submit to you and you alone. I offer you every situation in my life and invite you to take complete control. Pour out your Holy Spirit in all areas of my life. I look forward with confidence to the life-giving work you will do, and I thank you for it now, in Jesus' name. Amen."

A Final Blessing for You

"Father God, I bring before you every believer who has received the truth of your Word. Seal in their hearts every word that has been imparted, every spiritual revelation and reality that you have bestowed upon their minds and hearts.

"Let the precious treasure of your Gospel be sealed in their hearts. May they be changed this day. May they be inundated and infused with the very presence of the living God. Let the mind of Christ be in them.

"I bless you in your spirit. I bless you to know the Father and Son and Holy Spirit. I command revelation knowledge to flow into your life. I bless you in the name of the Father, the Creator of heaven and earth; and I bless you in the name of His Son, the Lord Jesus Christ, who shed His blood to save you from your sins. I bless you in the anointing of the Holy Spirit of God. May He fill your life to overflowing."

Chapter Six

LIVING FREE

Stand Fast in Liberty

S tand fast therefore in the liberty wherewith Christ hath made us free, and be not entangled again with the yoke of bondage (Galatians 5:1).

Paul wrote these words to the Galatians as a warning. They could not be passive and remain free. Freedom takes effort.

Peter gave the same warning when he said, *Be sober, be vigilant (1 Peter 5:8).* Your adversary, the devil, is still out there, trying to devour you. You must stand guard over your life.

> *Casting down imaginations, and every high thing that exalteth itself against the knowledge of God, and bringing into captivity every thought to the obedience of Christ (2 Corinthians 10:5).*

Much personal spiritual warfare takes place in your mind. You need to learn how to cast down imaginations, and thoughts, and every temptation that exalts itself against the Word of God. We are to walk in understanding of the Word and bring into captivity every thought of defeat, discouragement, depression or disease. We must take those sinful nudges by the throat and drag them to the throne of Christ.

We must make them obey the Word.

In the beginning was the Word, and the Word was with God, and the Word was God (John 1:1). You bring your wayward thoughts captive to the Bible. If they contradict the Word of God, they have to go.

Give them no place in your mind.

No Vacancy, Devil!

Ephesians 4:27 says, *Neither give place to the devil.* Remember, the word for place is "topos," which means "a position of opportunity." It also means "space limited by occupancy." That means all available space is full. There is no vacancy. The devil cannot get in because there is no room for him. When the devil tries to sit down on your bench, make sure the Holy Spirit is filling up the space.

Depression cannot get in ... disease cannot get in ... discouragement cannot get in, because you give them no ground.

Be filled with the Holy Spirit. Fill up your mind with words of faith.

You can only think one thought at a time. Your mind cannot hold two thoughts at once. You cannot think faith and doubt at the same time. Shove out the doubt. Give it no place.

Fill your mind with the Holy Spirit by filling it with the Word. Jesus said, *The words that I speak unto you, they are spirit, and they are life (John 6:63).* The words are spirit. The Bible is not a dead book. It is alive.

You cannot keep the devil out by filling your mind with any other words. They are dead words. Only the Word of God lives. Another way to keep the devil out is to pray in the spirit. Pray that heavenly, God-given language aloud. The devil does not understand it. He has to sit outside and wonder what you are talking about. Praying in the Holy Spirit jams the devil's radar. He cannot get messages through to you.

When the devil tries to attach his ugly works to you, or enter into you or enter into your house, or your family or your finances, you must be filled with the Holy Spirit. When he comes and finds your house full, there will be no place for him. There will be no room for his thoughts in your mind. There will be no room for his works in your body.

If he comes in and finds you watching or listening to worldly rock stars, he has found a window of opportunity. If he comes in and finds you watching a horror movie, he has found a place. If he arrives at your door and you are in a rage over what your neighbor has done, or what a co-worker has said about you, or what someone in the church nursery did, he will find a place.

Fill those places to overflowing so he cannot gain access.

The next time you and your spouse start to fight, kneel down together in front of the coffee table and make it an altar. You will stop fighting. You may not get to air your complaints, but before you know it you will be hugging one another and wondering what you were fighting over in the first place.

Some of you are tormented by your thoughts. Drive them out. Some of you are tormented by lust. Cast it out. Some of you are plagued with thoughts of murder, adultery or heresy. They are all intruders, so drive them out.

You may say, "I cannot do that."

The Greater One in you can.

Stay Out of the Devil's Territory

If you will stay out of the devil's territory, the evil one cannot touch you.

One of the reasons sickness hangs around your house is because you feed your spirit from the television, watching people do what you would never do. The Word says not to even mention those things which they do in secret, much less be entertained by them.

Dr. Sumrall was conducting a service when a woman came forward for deliverance from demonic power. He laid his hands on her and said, "Come out."

Suddenly, a man's voice came out of her. It said, "I don't have to leave. She wants me here. I have a right to be here."

Dr. Sumrall asked her, "Did you hear that?"

She answered. "I don't know what that was. I just came up here to be delivered because I can't sleep."

So he laid hands on her again and said, "Come out of her." And that voice boiled back up again, "I don't have to. She came on my territory. She gave me the right."

Dr. Sumrall asked her, "Is that right?"

She answered, "Oh, no. I don't know what that means."

And the voice came up again and said, "Yes, you do." And it announced that she had gone to an R-rated movie with pornography and swearing in it. "She came on my territory," it crowed. "I have a right to be here."

It is time to stop rationalizing sin. We have an unlimited capacity to make excuses for what we do. It is time to stop that and stay on our side of the line.

The Bible says, *What fellowship hath righteousness with unrighteousness? and what communion hath light with darkness? (2 Corinthians 6:14).*

The answer is — none.

Stay out of the devil's territory.

"I Will Destroy America!"

Dr. Sumrall was writing a book about the devil. He had titled it "Scarecrow." The manuscript was lying on his desk one night, when he had a vivid dream.

Dr. Sumrall was seventy-seven years old at the time. Although he had been in ministry for fifty-eight years, for the first time in his life he literally shook, and sweat broke out all over his body. An image appeared in a large television screen. It was a horrible face with bulging eyes.

It said, "I am not a scarecrow! I am Apollyon!"

The Book of Revelation speaks of Apollyon. It is one of the names of the Antichrist. It means destroyer.

And he told Dr. Sumrall, "I will destroy America.

I will do it through television. I will do it through music. I will do it through the occult spirit."

Can you see how this is happening in America? You cannot watch a comedy for more than three episodes before the scripts begin to mock God.

Watch what your children are watching. Even the cartoons are full of satanic symbols and mysticism. They are full of New Age philosophy.

How many rock and roll stations does your cable television network pump into your house? What are the songs about? Has anyone pulled up next to your car in traffic with rap music blasting out the windows? Have you heard the violent, murdering spirit poisoning the spirits of those who are listening?

The New Age movement is sweeping the nation. It is amazing to me how the West swallows what the East has been trying to get rid of for 500 years. To a Hindu, eternal salvation means getting out of the cycle of reincarnation — life, death, life, death, life, death. His whole quest is to break that cycle. Then the leaders dress it up and move it over here, and everyone wants to get involved in reincarnation. It is a fool's lie.

While they are looking for spirit guides, we have the real Spirit for a guide, and His unbreakable promise that He will lead us into all truth.

A Desensitized Mind

The devil is a deceiver. He knows that alert, vigilant Christians will recognize his attacks and stand against him. He is trying to bring us to a place of complacency where we will not recognize his voice or his work. He wants to desensitize your heart and mind to the point where sin no longer troubles you.

We have become desensitized to the point where we see murder and it does not affect us. We have seen so much of it on television that it does not have any impact on us. We do not even blink when people come on television and talk about gross sexual sins. We watch adultery all day long.

We listen to profanity pouring out of the television, out of the radio, out of the cassette or CD players. It is in the music. It is in the commentary. Gutter talk abounds, and we let it in. Our children pick it up, and we ask, "Where did they hear that?" And we put up with it.

Have you seen the way the designers want your ten-year-old daughter to dress? Have you seen the earrings dangling from the earlobes of boys? They did not learn that from the saints of God in the church!

We have become comfortable with what the world offers.

And here is a greater tragedy. It is bad enough to become so desensitized to the world that it does not concern you any longer, but this is worse: we become desensitized in the spirit realm.

We become numb in the spirit. A prophecy no longer affects us. Tongues no longer affect us. We used to weep when we heard "Amazing Grace," and now it means nothing to us. Our Bibles stayed closed where we put them down after church last week. Our prayer life flounders. Our power ebbs and the devil gains the advantage. There are intruders in the garden, and we do not even know they are there.

Start Your Engines!

I once saw a great ocean liner in the port of Hong Kong. Ships like that weigh thousands of tons and have huge boilers, engines that propel them across the ocean's currents.

And I saw a little tug boat go out there and hook a chain to that ocean liner. With no effort at all, the little tug boat started up its own engines and pulled that mighty ship behind it.

And I thought, it is so like Christians. It is easy to get drawn away.

The devil draws us away. He sails right up to us and puts on the chains that drag us into whatever snare he has set for us.

But if that ocean liner would suddenly start its engines and push the throttle in reverse, that little tug boat would get yanked backwards and dragged until it capsized and was lost.

The devil cannot take you in tow unless you shut your engines down. The Bible warns us that people can be *taken captive by him [the devil] at his will (2 Timothy 2:26)*. Taken captive by a defeated foe!

How can that happen? It happens because we are not alert. We are desensitized to the world. We are accustomed to living in an atmosphere of sin. We are used to the sound of the devil's voice, and we are easy prey for that seeking lion because we are not vigilant.

Guard Your Life

You must guard your life, and watch over your heart. Set armed guards around your spirit man. Arm them with the arsenal of the Word of God and do not let the enemy in.

Smith Wigglesworth was one of the greatest men of faith who ever lived. On one occasion he went to a friend's funeral. He walked up to the casket, jerked the body right out and shoved it up against the wall. He said, "I command you, in the name of Jesus, live!"

He let go of the body, and it fell right on the floor. He picked it back up, shoved it against the wall and said, "Live." The body fell again. He grabbed it a third time and said, "I told you once and I told you twice and I do not intend to tell you again. Now in the name of Jesus, live!"

The man opened his eyes and said, "Who is dead?"

Now, how did Smith Wigglesworth get like that?

Dr. Sumrall walked up to Smith Wigglesworth's house in London one day with a newspaper in his hand. When Smith Wigglesworth opened the door he saw the paper and said, "Leave it outside."

We not only let the newspaper in, we let fornicators in. We let adulterers in, witchcraft in, television shows that mock godly standards in.

He said, "We only read one book in this house."

So Dr. Sumrall left the paper outside. When he came in he asked, "How are you today?"

And Smith Wigglesworth replied: "Smith Wigglesworth never asks Smith Wigglesworth how Smith Wigglesworth feels today. I feel like an overcomer. I feel like I am the head and not the tail. I feel like I am the first and not the last. I am fully persuaded that what God has promised He is able also to perform. He is not a man that He should lie."

He was a man who guarded his life!

The Bible says, *Draw nigh to God, and he will draw nigh to you (James 4:8)*. God does not abide with casual acquaintances. He does not dwell with people who only read their Bible once a month and only pray in church. The power of God is not manifested in people who let their lives resemble the decayed state of the fallen world so closely there is hardly any difference.

We need to stop allowing the atmosphere of our homes and lives to be conducive for the manifestations of hell. Notify every devil that you know they are defeated. Announce to every spirit trying to gain entry that the Greater One lives in you. Give the devil no place!

Living Free

Paul wrote, *I fear, lest by any means, as the serpent beguiled Eve through his subtilty, so your minds should be corrupted from the simplicity that is in Christ (2 Corinthians 11:3)*.

Following Christ is not complicated. Guarding your heart is not difficult. It is a simple matter of getting back to Bible basics.

Let me offer you four simple steps to remaining free from the devil's chains.

Pray

This is absolutely the most important thing you can do to live free of the devil.

Prayer is our communication link with God. We need to stay within calling distance. When we get out of touch, we experience a breakdown in the lines of communication from headquarters. And when that happens, we become vulnerable to the enemy. We become motivated by our own deceived flesh. We begin to believe the lies the enemy bombards us with. Our ears become deafened to the still, small voice of the Holy Spirit.

There is a war on. We cannot afford to be out of touch with our Commander in Chief.

When you pray, you have access into the spirit realm where God is, and He will reveal to you the root cause of the battle you are facing.

Behind every situation you face are spiritual powers and rulers of darkness at work. Before you can tear down the strongholds the enemy has built in your home, your city and your nation, you must be able to recognize him and move your arsenal into place. The only way to do this is through prayer. Otherwise you are like a blindfolded soldier without a weapon, unable to see the enemy and lacking the firepower to destroy him.

The battle will be won first on your face before God, interceding, seeking wisdom and receiving direction.

Read the Bible

The Bible is God's voice to us. God's Word is eternal. It has no beginning of days and it has no ending of life. When the earth was without form, and when darkness covered the earth, the Word was.

God's Word does not change. It is the same yesterday, today and forever.

As soon as the disciples began to speak forth the Word in the name of Jesus, Satan tried to stop them. The disciples were thrown in jail, beaten and commanded not to speak or teach the Word.

Throughout the ages, men have ridiculed the Bible, banned it, burned it, tried to discredit it, twisted it and perverted it to fit their own carnal interpretations. But they failed to destroy it. It has survived every onslaught of hell and come down to us without corruption.

God and His Word are inseparable. The Word is unchangeable. The Word is alive. And the Word cannot fail.

Jesus said, *If ye abide in me, and my words abide in you, ye shall ask what ye will, and it shall be done unto you (John 15:7).* Let His words abide in you!

Go to Church

Jesus said, *And I say also unto thee, That thou art Peter, and upon this rock I will build my church; and the gates of hell shall not prevail against it (Matthew 16:18).*

Jesus did not say the gates of hell would not prevail against an evangelistic association or a teaching ministry. He said the gates of hell would not prevail against the church.

We are invading enemy-held territory with all the arsenal of God at our disposal. Yet while some are brandishing swords and spears, others are waving butter knives.

The anointing of God does not come free. You will not receive it by watching television. You will not receive it through reading <u>Time</u> magazine. You will not receive it isolating yourself from other Christians.

Forsake not the assembling of yourselves together (Hebrews 10:25).

We are in a battlefield, and we are not out here alone. Our fellow Christians are in the same trenches. Each of us must help our brothers and sisters stay on guard.

The church is not optional. It is not a social club. It is not a community service center. It is vital. We have an adversary who will destroy us unless we stand united through the church.

God is looking for Christians willing to commit to their local church. Your pastor covenants to preach the Gospel, pray for you and believe God for your miracles.

In return, you covenant to commit to the church, support your pastor and work together to reach the lost souls in your community.

Go to church. Go to church, and your children will not have to choose which parent to live with. Go to church, and you will not have to check into a drug rehabilitation center. Go to church, and you will not fall into every trap the devil sets for you.

Witness

When was the last time you told anyone how good God has been to you?

When was the last time you looked someone in the eye and told them, from the bottom of your heart, "I would be dead were it not for Jesus of Nazareth. I would be on my way to hell. My life would be a total shambles, but He found me. He took me in His arms. He washed me in His blood. He forgave me and I have eternal life. I have peace and joy that I never knew existed."

When was the last time you told someone how good He has been to you? Who have you told about the way He healed your body, lifted you out of depression, supplied your needs and saved your soul?

That is the word of your testimony. There is a lost world out there that needs to hear it.

Who can you tell?

Anyone God sends you to tell. Ask Him. Ask, "Father, give me someone prepared by your Spirit to tell about you. Let me tell them how good you have been to me. Let me tell them how wonderful it is to know Jesus as Savior."

Steady Pressure

The greatest strength in all the world is consistent, steady pressure.

I saw an example of this in the parking lot here at World Harvest Church. First, compacted gravel was spread on the ground. Asphalt was poured on top of the gravel to a depth of about eight inches. Then the steam rollers moved over it, flattening and rolling it smooth.

I could not punch through that asphalt with my fist. I would break my hand if I tried. The strongest man in the world could not do it.

But something else could.

In the spring, I noticed a little blade of grass. It had pushed through all those inches of pressed asphalt and was growing in the middle of the lot. It had punched through by applying consistent, steady pressure.

Satan is under your feet. Keep him there. Keep putting pressure on him. Keep pressure on sickness. Keep pressure on discouragement. Keep pressure on disease and poverty, doubt and unbelief.

Keep the pressure on the devil in your daily life.

Pray.

Read the Bible.

Go to church.

Give your testimony.

Keep the pressure on.

Your Right to be Free

Jesus entered the synagogue one day and encountered a woman with a spirit of infirmity. She had been bent over for eighteen years. He laid hands on her and said, *Woman, thou art loosed from thine infirmity (Luke 13:12)*, and she was immediately set free.

The ruler of the synagogue was indignant because he thought Jesus had broken the sabbath. And Jesus said, *Ought not this woman, being a daughter of Abraham, whom Satan hath bound, lo, these eighteen years, be loosed from this bond on the sabbath day? (v.16)*.

That phrase, *ought not she be loosed*, should actually be translated, "She has a right to be free."

Jesus was saying, "Satan had her bound, but she has a right to be free."

I want you to know that you have a right to be free. Jesus died for your right to be free. Jesus rose from the dead for your right to be free. Jesus defeated every diabolical devil of darkness for your right to be free.

And Jesus said, *If the Son therefore shall make you free, ye shall be free indeed (John 8:36)*.

NOTES

1. Bennett, William J., *The Index of Leading Cultural Indicators,* Washington: jointly published by Empower America, The Heritage Foundation and Free Congress Foundation, Vol. 2, March 1993, p.12.

2. "False Premises: The Assumptions that Hinder Ministry", Glendale: *Ministry Currents,* Vol. II, No. 4, October-December, 1992, p.2.

3. Bennett, *Cultural Indicators,* p.12.

4. *Prophetic Observer,* National Center for Health Statistics chart, Southwest Radio Church, March 1994, p.2 L-736.

5. Bennett, *Cultural Indicators,* p.9.

6. Ibid., p.10.

7. Newman, Barclay, *A Concise Greek-English Dictionary of the New Testament,* London: United Bible Societies, 1971, p.192.

8. Arndt, William F. and Gingrich, F. Wilbur, *A Greek-English Lexicon of the New Testament and Other Early Christian Literature,* Chicago and London: The University of Chicago Press, 1979, p.855.

9. Moulton, Harold K., *The Analytical Greek Lexicon Revised,* Grand Rapids: Zondervan Publishing House, 1978, p.30.

10. Ibid., p.12.

11. Ibid., p.12.

12. "Girls' Suicides Baffle Friends," Setauket, NY: *New York Times,* December 5, 1993, p.10A.

13. "San Ramon Boy's Suicide Puzzles Teachers, Peers," San Jose: *Mercury News Wire Services,* Bay Area News in Brief, May 5, 1994, p.9B.

14. "Boy, 11, Shoots Self Outside His School," San Jose: *Mercury News Wire Services,* State News in Brief, April 14, 1994, p.3B.

15. Sanchez, Sandra, "Assisted Suicide Ban Ruled Illegal," *USA Today,* December 14, 1993, p.1A.

16. Daniel Schorr, "TV Violence - What We Know But Ignore," *AFA Journal,* January 1994, p.5.

17. "Family Slayings," *USA Today,* May 27, 1994, p.A1.

18. "When Rage Turns Into Mass Murder," *U.S. News and World Report,* July 30, 1984, p.14.

19. Anita Manning, "Gunshot Kills One U.S. Child Every Two Hours," *USA Today,* January 21, 1994, p.A1.

20. Bennett, *Cultural Indicators,* p.10.

21. Dobson, James and Bauer, Gary L., *Children at Risk,* Dallas: Word Publishing, 1990, p.2.

22. "Abortion Aftercare," *Ameritech Yellow Pages,* Ameritech Publishing, Inc., 1993, p.2.

23. "Roe's Momentous Anniversary: Undoing Republican Rulings, Clinton Lifts Ban on Abortions," *The New York Times,* January 24, 1994, p.A4.

24. Abbott, Karen, "A Dollar a Day Keeps the Babies Away," *Rocky Mountain News,* December 2, 1993, p.7D.

25. Brown, Floyd G., "Life and Death in Arkansas," *The National Review,* April 26, 1993, p.38-39.

26. VanBiema, David, "For the Love of Kids," *Time Magazine,* November 1, 1993, p.51.

27. "Young Defendants," *USA Today,* May 27, 1994, p.A1.

28. Gross, Jane, "Where Boys Will Be Boys and Adults are Bewildered," *The New York Times,* March 29, 1993, p.1A.

29. Fields, Suzanne, "Listening to Elder and Say No," *The Washington Times,* July 15, 1993, p.G1.

30. Statistical Summary, The Ohio State University Library Administration, June 23, 1994 printout.

31. "Ohio State OK's Gay Couples in Family Housing," *Chicago Tribune,* May 14, 1993, p.12.

32. Dobson, James, "Hamilton Square Baptist Church," *1993 in Review,* Colorado Springs: Focus on the Family, p.3.

33. Glamser, Deean, "Gay Pastors Find Open Arms, Hearts in Seattle," *USA Today,* August 22, 1994, p.A3.

34. Charen, Monda, "Being Homosexual and Bisexual is Fashionable on High School Campuses," *AFA Journal,* July, 1994, p.17.

35. "Fatal Addiction: <u>Ted Bundy's final interview with Dr. James Dobson</u>," Colorado Springs: Focus on the Family, 1989. 56 minutes.

36. Carelli, Richard, "Administration Softens Its Definition of Hard Core Child Pornography," *Associated Press,* September 23, 1993.

37. Center for Disease Control, May 31, 1994.

38. Larson, Bob, "Islam," *Larson's New Book of Cults,* Wheaton: Tyndale House, 1982, p.101.

39. <u>Ibid</u>., "Jehovah Witnesses," p.268,269.

40. <u>Ibid</u>., "Scientology," p.366.

41. <u>Ibid</u>., "Mormonism," p.308.

42. "Should Cigarettes Be Outlawed?," *U.S. News & World Report,* April 18, 1994, p.35.

43. *USA Today,* March 21, 1992.

44. Arterburn, Stephen and Burns, Jim, *Drug Proof Your Kids,* Pomona: Focus on the Family Publishing, 1989.

45. "Number of Crimes Committed," *The Prophetic Observer,* March 1994, p.3.

46. Bennett, *Cultural Indicators,* p.4.

47. "Lifetime Likelihood of Victimization" Technical Reports, U.S. Department of Justice, Bureau of Justice Statistics, March, 1987.

48. Larson, Bob, *Straight Answers on the New Age,* Nashville: Thomas Nelson Publishers, 1989, p.165.

49. Ibid., p.174.

50. Levine, Art, "Mystics on Main Street," *U.S. News & World Report,* February 1987, Vol. 102, No. 5, p.67.

51. Jefferson, Graham, "Astrologers Chart Their Ascendencies," *USA Today,* July 18, 1986, p.1D.

52. Ibid., p.10.

53. Anderson, Neil T. and Russo, Steve, Eugene: *The Seduction of Our Children,* Harvest House, 1991, p.67.

54. Ibid.

55. Ibid.

56. Larson, "Spiritualisam/Spiritism," *New Book of Cults,* p.393.

57. Simonds, Bob, *Citizens for Excellence Newsletter,* National Association of Christian Educators, May 1990, pp.2-5.

58. National Association of Christian Educators, *Citizens for Excellence Newsletter,* May 1990, pp.2-5.

59. Larson, "Witchcraft," *New Book of Cults,* p.464.

60. <u>Ibid</u>., "Voodoo/Santeria," pp.459,460.

61. Dictionary of the Words in The Hebrew Bible, *Strong's Exhaustive Concordance,* Grand Rapids: Baker Book House, p.52.

About the Author

Rod Parsley began his ministry as an energetic 19 year old, in the backyard of his parents' Ohio home. The fresh, "old-time Gospel" approach of Parsley's delivery immediately attracted a hungry, God-seeking audience. From the 17 people who attended the first backyard meeting, the crowds grew rapidly.

Today, as the pastor of Columbus, Ohio's, 5200-seat World Harvest Church, Parsley oversees World Harvest's preschool-12 Christian Academy; World Harvest Bible College; numerous church-sponsored outreaches; and Breakthrough, World Harvest Church's daily and weekly television broadcast, currently available to 96% of the populations of the United States and parts of Canada.

Rod Parsley also serves as Dr. Lester Sumrall's personal assistant in directing the End-Time Joseph "Feed the Hungry" program.

To contact the author write:

Rod Parsley
Breakthrough
P.O. Box 32932
Columbus, Ohio 43232-0932
24 Hour Prayer Line: (614) 837-3232
TDD: (614) 327-8337

Books by Rod Parsley

Repairers of the Breach

The Commanded Blessing

I'm Glad You Asked

Renamed and Redeemed

*My Promise is the Palace,
So What am I Doing in the Pit?*

The Backside of Calvary

God's Answer to Insufficient Funds

From Tribulation to Triumph

Holiness: Living Leaven Free

Praise and Worship

Serious Survival Strategies for Victory

Financial Abundance

*If God Hadn't Wanted to Heal You,
He Shouldn't Have*

New Direction

*Strengthening the Roots of Your
Family Tree*

*A product list is available for the many
audio and video series Parsley has produced.*

Available From:
World Harvest Church
P.O. Box 32903
Columbus, Ohio 43232-0903
(614) 837-1990